BUILDING POSITIVE B

PRAISE FOR BUILD BEHAVIOUR

This is a brilliant, honest, brave, well-informed and eminently practical book. Graham has drawn from his wealth of experience in mainstream schools and alternative provision as well as his deep knowledge, to produce a really helpful guide to working with pupils who present what we sometimes call "challenging behaviour" (Graham prefers the term "dysregulated.")

Giving many examples from his own broad experience, Graham, who openly admits he didn't always get it right himself, explains how and why a sequential approach can work to produce "calmer children, calmer classrooms, more learning." Every now and then he interrupts himself with a "Pause for Thought" question, inviting us to reflect on our own practice.

Particularly timely in 2020, as our children return from lockdown, this is a book for all seasons. I wish it had been around 30 years ago, because I too didn't always get it right.

JOHN COSGROVE, RETIRED HEADTEACHER, AUTHOR

In this new post COVID era. It is important to have key voices guiding us on how best to support our young people. Within a mainstream setting, we are faced with returning vulnerable children with challenging behaviours that we have not supported before or have no experience working with.

Through this book I have been able to gain knowledge on this area and plan for our returning pupils using the approaches and examples laid out in it's pages. In a time when budgets are tight and children have been without support for a significant period of time it is important to use approaches based in evidence, that will support the whole child, to be able to move forward in the world, not just within school.

That is the message of this book and one that I think is vital reading for anyone working in mainstream: TA, teacher and SLT alike.

PAIGE BRIGGS, ASSISTANT HEAD, SENCO, EDGEWICK COMMUNITY PRIMARY SCHOOL

Graham Chatterley's book *Building Positive Behaviour.* Is a good read for those wanting to develop a school culture based on connection and a relational approach to supporting 'troubled' children and young people.

Graham is very passionate about schools getting this right in order that those with the greatest barriers to engagement with learning are successful. This is evident in every page of the book.

The strongest element of the book is the use of individual case studies of children and young people that Graham has actually worked with. These really help the reader to understand the barriers that they have faced and the behaviour that these present. It also provides us with some signposts for meeting their needs and helping them to achieve and therefore improve their life chances.

MICHAEL PURCHES, RETIRED HEADTEACHER, EDUCATION CONSULTANT

This practical guide is palatable reading for any audience, regardless of training or sophistication, and the reader cannot help but feel more hopeful by it's conclusion.

The invaluable resource provides a sophisticated technique for professionals working with young people with challenging behaviour. Graham provides a friendly, conversational style that addresses the reader teacher-to-teacher. It explains a variety of strategies in a jargon-free way that is both clear and readable without being patronising.

The overriding tone is one of empathy. The insights are patently coming from someone who has experienced all of this himself. It helps you stand back and look at why children might be behaving the way they are, and the ways in which you might act to help them; that can only be a good thing.

DEE MILBERY, DIRECTOR OF PBT LTD, BEHAVIOUR CONSULTANT

For Ethan, Morgan, Max and Daniel

In memory of Simon, the original form tutor Dad

CONTENTS

Introduction		1
1.	**There is another way**	11
	Believing it can be different	14
	Relationships and systems	15
2.	**Do we want more of the same?**	19
	The minority	20
	Set up to fail	23
	You can't fix everything with a hammer	25
	Small humans	26
	What do we see?	27
	Fight fire with water	29
3.	**Triage : Why triage is vital**	31
	Being proactive	33
	What are we triaging?	34
	How best to triage	37
	New rules	39
4.	**So what is the Sequential Approach?**	45

	Rebuilding safety	46
	Regaining trust	48
	Teaching Re-regulation	51
	Building Belonging	52
	Fostering Courage	54
5.	**STAGE 1 - Why does safety always come first?**	57
	The perception of threat	59
	Trapped	60
	Validate don't fix	62
	What is it we need to do?	62
	Picking up the pieces	67
6.	**How do we create safety?**	77
	Positive touch is a cornerstone of relationships	79
	Touch as a communication tool for pupils	80
	Touch as a communication tool for staff	82
	Children instigating vs avoiding touch	83
	Creating safety through touch	86
	Rebuilding safety resources	88
	MEET AND GREET	*89*
	PHYSICALLY DISTANCED MEET AND GREET	*90*
	NURTURING POSITIVE TOUCH	*91*

	MEET AND GREET ROULETTE 92
	HANDSHAKE COMPETITION 93
7.	**Working <u>WITH</u> children** 95
	Challenge vs support 97
	What do we do when they fall below expectations? 101
	Creating emotional resilience 103
	Getting their voices heard 111
	Coaching circles 112
	LIVE - active listening 113
8.	**STAGE 2 - Will you keep coming back?** 117
	We let them down, so how are we going to fix it? 123
	You have to matter 129
	Every interaction counts 131
	Building trust through repair 132
9.	**STAGE 3 - Why do we need to teach self-regulation** .. 139
	Dysregulation as aggression 141
	Anger suppression 143
	The forgotten children 144
	Use it or lose it 147
	All aboard! Last stop aggression 150
	Getting them off the train 152

7

	Changing tracks	155
10.	**Supporting re-regulation**	157
	Individual interventions	159
	Eskape	168
	Re-regulation resources	169
	3.1 READY TO LEARN MORNINGS	*170*
	3.2 RE-REGULATION USING PHYSICAL ACTIVITY	*171*
	3.2.1 PHYSICAL ACTIVITY - GAME	*172*
	3.2.2 PHYSICAL ACTIVITY - HIGH INTENSITY .	*173*
	3.2.3 PHYSICAL ACTIVITY - LOW INTENSITY ...	*174*
	3.3 RE-REGULATION USING ART & CRAFT ..	*175*
	3.4 SENSORY RE-REGULATION	*176*
	3.4.1 SENSORY ACTIVITY - TOUCH	*177*
	3.5 MINDFULNESS RE-REGULATION	*178*
	3.6 MUSIC RE-REGULATION	*179*
	Becoming unstuck	180
	Re-regulation conclusion	181
11.	**STAGE 4 - Fear of rejection**	183
	Boundaries	186
	Social skills	188

	The power of play	189
	Reject first	190
	Mask 1 - The Rejector	191
	Mask 2 - The Manipulator	195
	Mask 3 - The Class Clown	198
	Every child needs to belong	201
	Teach social skills	206
	Selfish, thoughtless & dangerous	207
	Social isolation as punishment	209
	Social isolation as support	211
12.	**Stage 5 - Brave learners**	**213**
	The test	214
	Red flags	216
	The camouflaged	217
	The perfectionist	222
13.	**Behaviour is communication**	**227**
	Let them fly	230
	Conclusion	235

INTRODUCTION

What does your school want to achieve when fully returning to school?

Are we happy to return to how things were or have we got a chance to change for the better?

I believe we potentially have more dysregulated children than ever returning to school and we have 2 options;

We can accept and follow the guidance of the DfE and government behavlour advisor to focus on the behaviours, rules and consequences. Maybe get back to where we were.

Or we can understand the reality that more is required and take a human approach one that will not only help us to navigate the storm that is potentially coming but also has some very positive long term side effects;

- **Calmer Children** - significant reduction in distressed/dysregulated children
- **Calmer Classrooms** - significant reduction in disruption to lessons

- **More Learning** - significant increase in learning potential for all due to better executive functioning

> Shouldn't these be the outcomes every school is striving for?

A giant pause button has been hit on education. Now is a perfect opportunity for a reset or a re-think.

In the two decades I have been a teacher the world has changed: employment has changed, children have changed but education has remained the same for far longer. Both in how children are expected to learn and how they are expected to behave. We have more than 50 years of new knowledge about these 2 things, so how can the Education system still be using the same model? I would wholeheartedly welcome changes to the curriculum, but my belief is that this isn't as big a priority as improving the approach to behaviour. If we want real positive change this is where we start.

This book is for any educator who believes that the culture could be better, any leader who believes too many children aren't being successful and any adult who asks themselves the question; why do children behave the way they do and how can I help them?

I have always shared my specialist SEMH work with mainstream counterparts and always believed it can be replicated in every school. With the right culture and the right scaffold all children can thrive and learn. I believe the sequential approach in this book is that scaffold and I believe there is no better time than right now.. The information, examples and resources along the way will aim to show how it can be achieved.

WHY WILL THE SEQUENTIAL APPROACH HELP?

The Sequential Approach will identify what causes challenging behaviour. By identifying where a child's difficulties begin and working in a sequence we can equip that child with everything they need to manage school life. This book will increase understanding of the motivators of challenging behaviour and this understanding will change how that behaviour is perceived. The increase in empathy that this creates will give our more vulnerable and often most challenging pupils the safety, belonging and courage to thrive in our schools. We have an opportunity to take a culture from a position of where most succeed, to where **all** can succeed.

MY EXPERIENCES

I will give many examples of children I have worked with and I will use some of the most extreme examples from some of my most challenging pupils to emphasise the impact. Often the interventions I used were time consuming and heavily resourced in the beginning and probably very difficult to achieve in a mainstream setting. However our interventions were years late, following many avoidable failures and having to unlearn the behaviours they had developed to hide their difficulties. If work similar to what we did had been done earlier and in the sequence I'm suggesting in this book I believe the majority of the work we did would never have been necessary for those children.

My early teaching career was a struggle, from Initial Teacher Training making me believe authority and discipline were what I needed, witnessing great practice but not understanding at the time why it was great. What followed was working in schools which were very behaviour focussed and behaviour was controlled via rewards and sanctions. I was regularly left not understanding why things that worked for others didn't work for me.

Then at a point of being close to leaving the profession, finding out the power of relationships and how they could be used positively. To working with incredibly skilled de-escalators who taught me how by learning 'what a child feels' I can understand what drives their behaviours. Finally to a twilight INSET session with Lisa Wisher where she opened up my eyes to the impact that experiences have on the feelings, before they drive any behaviour. She sent me down a rabbit hole I have never got out of.

WHY WE MUST SEE MORE THAN BEHAVIOUR

It isn't that the DfE guidance is wrong, it just doesn't offer enough. The work schools have done in 2020 they deserve more. Boundaries and rules are important, but they are a small part of what our children need. Boundaries, structures and rules should underpin a much more relationships based approach. If we only see the behaviour they display then we don't see the child. There is a purpose to that behaviour, if we understand what it is we can change it. I wrote this book to offer what I believe is missing.

The mis-perception of a child's behaviour is an incredibly easy thing. Especially with the masking ability of some of our young people. It's so important to have understanding because we will often see it completely different.

CLAYTON'S SPOONS

One of the biggest ever mis-perceptions of behaviour I ever experienced came quite early in my SEMH career. I was in a meeting with the assistant head in her first floor office. I was thrown off the conversation by some shouting outside, then much to our surprise a small boy with black hair and glasses appeared at the window. When we calmly asked what he was doing on the roof; fully expecting him to be in crisis, he very calmly replied "I'm just collecting spoons!" before handing us half a dozen spoons. A couple of staff were shouting up at him telling him to "get down" and what would happen if he didn't. He was accused of avoiding work and absconding class.

It was clear that the staff weren't in control of the situation, had decided he was behaving this was to avoid work and due to their own escalation Clayton was starting to shout things back at them. We were able to persuade him to come in through the window but were fully expecting something negative to have happened that had prompted his going on the roof.

It turns out that Clayton had a really good relationship with the school cook. He had got himself a yoghurt but there were no spoons left. When he had asked for another one she had said she was really sorry and really frustrated but they kept going missing. She said she would have to go buy some more because they were disappearing. Clayton said he accepted this but didn't like seeing her upset. When he left the dining room to go onto yard he saw one of the older boys had smuggled a yoghurt out of the dining room and then thrown his spoon onto the roof.

Clayton decided he would go and get it and see if there were any more. He had found some more but not before staff had found him on the roof. He was scared he would be in trouble if he got down so stayed on the roof. When he started getting shouted at for what he believed was helping he had gotten abusive to the staff.

It was the wrong action for the right reason. Should we be rushing to punish a child for breaking rules when they are doing something kind. We had a brilliant opportunity to praise the intention but challenge the behaviour. This was a behavioural mistake but it was also a learning opportunity. Knowing the motivation behind Clayton's behaviour gave us this. Looking at the behaviour in isolation would have resulted in a serious consequence and a message to Clayton that kindness will be punished. This is why context and understanding have to be our priority.

ORIGIN

'The Sequential Approach' is a combination of 2 other major influences on my career and the ethos I have; Abraham Maslow and Dr Bruce Perry. Maslow's 1954 hierarchy shows the importance of putting building blocks in place in order to progress. It's been changed and questioned over the last 70 years but for me the principles are still as vital as they ever were and have been fundamental in my work with children. Whilst reading 'The boy who was raised as a dog' by Dr Bruce Perry made me believe as a teacher that every child can be helped. It's why I get annoyed when children get written off and also why I make bold statements about **all** children benefiting from what I'm suggesting. Bruce Perry talks about a neurosequential approach to repairing trauma. The importance of having each element led by the child and at their own pace. Not trying to push too far too fast or run before we can walk. These principles are exactly what children need to overcome any adverse experiences.

What also makes this Sequential Approach so accessible to schools is that many of the aspects are already being done. At a time when budgets and staffing are tight, making changes can seem impossible, but changing cultures and approaches doesn't cost more money or require extra resources. It's less about gaining new knowledge as looking differently at the knowledge we already have.

When I was Pastoral Lead I realised we were doing all the elements but sometimes in the wrong order, or we were moving on too soon before something was embedded.

JAY THE SABOTEUR

Jay was an angelic looking Year 1 boy. Surfer blonde hair, bright blue eyes and cheeky smile, he looked like he could do no wrong.

However I first observed Jay in a PE lesson where he was struggling immensely. Not able to sit still, interrupting, spoiling the games of others and lashing out. Midway through the lesson Jay asked to leave and the Teaching Assistant took him to class. As soon as he was away from peers he relaxed, started to talk about world maps on the wall, what animals lived in different countries etc. Then the other children returned from PE and he became very heightened again.

The school were doing everything they could think of to try and support J but were doing too much all at once and that's why it was breaking down. They were trying to teach social skills before teaching self-regulation, and J was breaking it down . He could often work well in small groups led by the teacher but as soon as he left that space the problems would start again.

Jay was stuck in a loop. He was desperate to belong but constantly feared rejection. The only way to control it was to be the one who rejects. Even though it doesn't make him happy it's better than waiting for it to happen.

"The certainty of misery is preferable to the misery of uncertainty" Virginia Satir.

Other children were rightly wary of Jay. Yes, he lashed out and spoiled games but most importantly from the perspective of the other children he was unpredictable. He seemed to be friendly one minute but aggressive the next and children find this very difficult to understand. Being hypervigilant Jay would sense this wariness as an oncoming rejection and sabotage potential friendships before they could go wrong. Therefore any progress made in the small group was forgotten the second he went to defence mode.

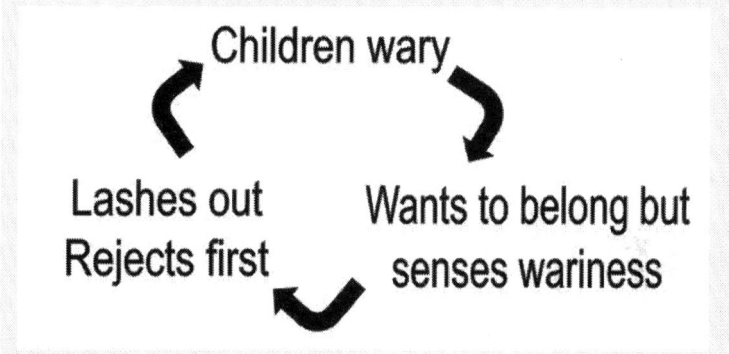

```
         ↗ Children wary ↘

  Lashes out        Wants to belong but
  Rejects first  ↙  senses wariness
```

The school were doing all the right things to create a safe environment, to build trust with adults, and social skills work. Problem was he couldn't trust the other children because they didn't trust him, they couldn't trust him because he pushed them away as a defence. Jay was stuck!

How many children we work with are stuck in their own cycles?

How many children returning post Covid 19 will be stuck?

In Jay's case, once he has the skills to regulate, the loop will be broken. The skills can be taught, many schools already are, but how do we ensure children are ready to learn them?

Chapter 1

THERE IS ANOTHER WAY

"When a flower doesn't bloom, you fix the environment in which it grows, not the flower" - Alexander Den Heijer

In 2014 OFSTED estimated an hour a day is lost due to poor behaviour. In an attempt to combat this there has been a rise in zero tolerance approaches. My questions are these;

1. How much of the misbehaviour is actually a child being dysregulated?

2. How much of this misbehaviour is masking other difficulties? (Sound processing/ visual processing/ ASD/ ADHD/Trauma)

3. Do we do enough to find out the cause of the behaviours or do we just manage the symptoms?

When the answer to question 3 is no. So, if we state a shortage of time being the reason for this, but does it not make more sense to find a cure than to keep treating symptoms?

> **Pause for thought-** would you describe your setting as proactive or reactive when it comes to behaviour?

For example:- Let's say every morning children in my class drink milk and every afternoon the same child is sick. If a child was physically sick everyday they would visit the Doctor. The Doctor would investigate why and probably run some tests. The results might find out they have an intolerance to dairy.

At this point I have 5 choices;

Option 1 is to remove the child at times of milk.

Option 2 is to remove the milk from everyone.

Option 3 continue to give the milk but provide anti-sickness medication

Option 4 is to give everyone else milk but the child nothing or something different

Option 5 give them all non-dairy milk

Looking at the first three options they seem ridiculous choices. Would you exclude a child from class for being Lactose intolerant? Should everyone miss out because one has a different need? Would you keep doing the same thing even though you know it causes harm and then try to deal with the aftermath?

No way! So why are all these things perfectly acceptable strategies when it comes to behaviour?

Option 4 is a viable option but the children; especially for the older ones, their desire to be seen as the same as everyone else is a huge factor. Plus should they really miss out because they have something going on that they have zero control over?

Option 5 seems sensible and reasonable. It doesn't seem time consuming. It doesn't seem like a big inconvenience. A small change to the way things are done and the content to save the distress and time down the line. A change that doesn't single out and goes largely unnoticed.

The priority is to find out why the child is being sick. Then when it is identified nearly all people would opt straight for option 5. The idea that we don't find out why the child is being sick doesn't seem to make sense!

So why is it that when poor behaviour is the symptom we delay the investigation? Why do we go through all the other options first? Why is our focus not on the cause?

If we were to take the DfE guidance literally they take it a step further with their own two options;

Option 6 is to reward them for drinking the milk but give them a consequence if they are sick.

Option 7 is to punish refusal to drink the milk.

If we treated children this way for their physical health there would be huge questions to answer!

BELIEVING IT CAN BE DIFFERENT

In February 2020 I attended an event in Leeds for the 'Lose the Booths' Campaign. It started with Paul Dix, author of 'When the adults change everything changes' and is trying to raise awareness of the damage Isolation Booths cause to children when they are used as punishment. It was filled with speakers of successful schools who don't use isolation booths and avoid a zero tolerance approach.

Now avoiding the politics of that issue which has really polarised education; the thing that really struck me about the day was the number of people who were there because of curiosity. People who were at the event having been told there is no other way and isolation booths are essential to the discipline and behaviour systems in their school, that these people have great ideas but ones that could never possibly work or that they are reckless, hate rules and let children run riot.

However, despite all the messages to the contrary; from their initial teacher training when everything was made about being an authority figure, to all the current messages coming from the behaviour advisor/DfE and then most importantly what their current schools and probably their teaching experience had told them; these people still attended the event. They attended because in their gut they weren't happy with what they were being asked to do, they knew too many children were failing and so they wanted to support children differently. They were looking for a different way.

They left that day believing there is another way!

RELATIONSHIPS AND SYSTEMS

The big argument of having a more human/relationship based approach is that they are against systems and rules. This is simply not true.

I was recently told that 'systems are more important than the relationships'. This is also not true.

Relationships and systems run alongside each other. Systems are good, consistency is good but there will be those that struggle with the systems;

- Children who struggle to regulate and manage overwhelming feelings
- Children who mask underlying difficulties with their poor behaviour
- Children whose shame makes them believe they are no good, that they are going to fail anyway so they might as well have some control over it.

The system alone doesn't work for these children; they need the relationship.

> *"Relationships are the agents of change and the most powerful therapy is human love."* Bruce Perry

It is vital that the relationship is at least of equal importance. This is an approach adopted by many schools and seems a sensible middle ground for schools to take. Somewhere in between the harshness of zero tolerance and the perception of children running riot. I believe that in normal circumstances this is probably an effective way to run a school.

The 2 hands of discipline by Kim Golding

Hand One
Provides connection with warmth and nurture

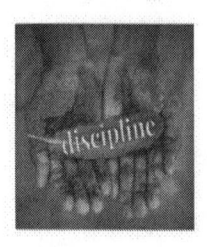

Hand Two
Provides structure, supervision and boundaries

Whilst I agree that we need to be explicit with new and existing rules to ensure safety. How we inform the children of these rules is crucial, as is the approach we take when behavioural mistakes are made. I believe that the introduction of these rules and expectations must be done in a more Hand One kind of way.

Now post Covid 19 we are likely to have more children who can't regulate, more children who need the relationship. It's hard to remember things when worried and scared. Punishment for getting it wrong will only add to this.

> *'If there is too much heat around boundary-setting, then the climate created will be adolescent-unfriendly and vulnerable-adolescent-toxic. It will be counter-productive; escalating'* Mary Meredith

Other than saving time, I don't believe there is anything to be gained from big formal assemblies listing rules or every instruction starting with 'don't' or threats of what will happen if they forget and accidentally hug each other or walk the wrong way or touch their face. Better behaviour will follow better relationships. Some of which will need to be rebuilt for reasons I will come to. We need to introduce the new rules but we don't need the formality or fear. We have an opportunity to discuss the importance of the rules in form groups, in PHSE sessions or nurture activities. Less pressure, more human and more understanding of why, with a payoff of finding out what children feel about it. An opportunity to learn about their experiences and why they might be struggling with their behaviour. We can still have limits on behaviour but they underpin empathy and understanding. This is what is lacking from the DfE guidance.

Tom Bennett talks about behaviour not being an afterthought when referring to his 'Rebooting Behaviour after Lockdown' document. However it has no mention of having any forethought about what causes challenging behaviour. If our solution for that behaviour is threatening or giving sanctions after the behaviour has occurred, then it is by very definition an afterthought that is being encouraged. You wouldn't attempt to remove a tree without digging out the root yet this document doesn't equip us with a spade.

> **Pause for thought** - are both hands working together in your setting?

Chapter 2

DO WE WANT MORE OF THE SAME?

Education seems to be in a rush to return to where it was. Back to normality, but my question is why do we want to get back to where we were?

We have an opportunity to go somewhere different, and I'm not referring to curriculum changes, assessment changes or accountability changes, (Which many argue are many years out of date and in serious need of an overhaul) I'm talking about how we treat pupils, how we understand pupils, how we listen to pupils and how we communicate with pupils.

There are exceptions but for a great many Teachers the second they walk into university it is a message of 'the teacher must control and the children must conform'. Authority is the key: enforcing systems, rewards and sanctions will allow you to be in control, have discipline, manage your classroom. The problem is that all these things are extrinsic. The **majority** will behave for the reward or fear of consequence, the **majority** will respect the teacher and follow the rules regardless.

However;

The majority will feel safe in school because they have no reason to feel unsafe.

The majority will trust adults because they have no reason not to.

The majority will be able to regulate their emotions because they were taught to self-soothe as an infant and have been taught it's ok to feel things.

The majority will have good peer relationships because they know how to play, feel safe interacting with others and although they care what their peers think they don't fear rejection from them.

The majority are using the correct part of their brain to process information and are willing to take risks in their learning.

THE MINORITY

What about the minority?

- What about the children who don't feel safe?
- What about the children whose experience of adults is, they can't be trusted?
- What about the children who were never taught to self-soothe during infancy so don't know how to regulate big emotions?

- What about children who don't know how to play and are consumed by the constant internal battle between wanting to belong but fearing failure?

Do we expect these children to be able to concentrate, process information effectively, negotiate the school environment and take risks with their learning?

Does it matter as long as they conform?

We have just had to create an environment in school where some vulnerable children, who usually struggle have thrived in school because of bubbles. Yes the groups were smaller which isn't sustainable long term, but the more relational approach, less pressurised learning environment and more play are. Children who are regularly in trouble for their behaviour and seen as challenging or unpleasant have been different and better behaved in extremely difficult circumstances. If the change of environment has done so much to help this child then isn't returning to exactly how things were a missed opportunity for positive change.

> **Pause for thought** - how has the different environment affected those who have been attending?

What if in this post Covid 19 world the minority just got bigger? What if the 5% of children who never feel safe, who don't trust, who can't manage their emotions or feel rejected is now 20%, or 30%, or 50%. Is strong systems/rules/boundaries going to be enough if we have more dysregulated children?

Many schools rely on Pastoral support outside the classroom. Pastoral teams can pick up a small minority, they are often skilled enough to repair conflict, to offer a place of safety and a listening ear but pastoral support is part of the system which will soon become overwhelmed if dysregulated children double. If a school has relied on a system where Pastoral support is external to the classroom, they pass on this vital role so they 'can teach'. They miss out so many important elements our more vulnerable children need. There will always be pupils who need the human, they need the pastoral approach in the classroom and it can't be seperate.

Pastoral support is a huge part of teaching small humans. Without it we are just inputting data.

Children aren't animals to be trained by fear or treats, or robots always processing information without feeling. They don't need a trainer or a data inputter. They start as small humans who make human mistakes, they need a human teacher who understands, shares their own feelings and own mistakes and teaches them how to learn from those mistakes. Without this teaching they become bigger humans making the same mistakes over and over.

Authoritarian systems often get results. I'm not denying it. When we train children with rules and strict boundaries it will achieve compliance for the majority. It's what we are told from the very beginning of our careers but I don't believe it's enough, especially without the relationship.

SET UP TO FAIL

I nearly didn't make it to being a teacher. I was close to failing in my 2nd year. I was told relentlessly about respect and authority and in trying to gain this I didn't have any personality as a teacher. I didn't attempt to build relationships with my pupils because I was afraid of being too friendly and losing my authority. I scraped through and looking back I'm not sure I deserved to. I think I was saved in that final year because of 2 things. One was the fellow course member I was on placement with and the other was the placement coinciding with the class residential.

JAMIE'S LESSON

Jamie was the crazy Welshman on my course. From deep in the Rhondda valleys he had charisma by the bucketload and was mad as a box of frogs.

I never saw him teach but I saw his interactions with children outside of the classroom; joking around with them, hi fives, playful teasing. It went against the messages I had. Whether I'd misinterpreted them or not I was worried that if I imitated this I couldn't pull it off or worse it would impact my authority.

The fact was though it was clear he was sailing through the course and I was struggling so I would be stupid not to take heed. We happened to be on teaching practice when the school residential came. It was perfect because it puts you into positions where it is impossible not to show your personality. The relationships I built with my class on that residential and built on during break times back in school are what I believe got me through my course. I realise now my classroom management wasn't done inside the classroom, those interactions were me investing in the children during their time and what I got back was their investment during mine.

I took a while to catch on but Jamie understood this from the beginning. He went on to become an Executive Head in South Wales which is of no surprise.

However it still meant that when I started a job and was on my own I was totally unprepared and nearly failed my NQT year, before I finally found a style that suited me which I'll talk about later.

YOU CAN"T FIX EVERYTHING WITH A HAMMER!

Most children are nails. A blunt instrument like a hammer will give you the desired result. The force with which you hit them can vary but the nail will go in. The problem is not all children are nails, some are screws. You can usually hammer in a screw but it never works properly and some will break or split the wood. These children require a different approach and a different tool.

What happens to these children when the hammer doesn't work and we don't own a screwdriver?

There's no doubt fear is a strong motivator for most, but at what cost? You are always going to have those you can't scare; those that have life experiences that make your detention feel like a walk in the park, those that every second of every day is fear and anxiety so what you threaten makes no difference. Not forgetting there will always be those that after years of failure believe they are bad, act the way you expect them to and get the punishment they deserve. It is so important we don't perpetuate shame in children. Breaking through the defences of these children may require another tool. We may need to drill into the hard exterior first before we screw it in.

> **Pause for thought** - how often is the full set of tools being used in your setting?

SMALL HUMANS

Also lets not forget those children who are so afraid to show their feelings for fear of consequence they are permanently in a freeze response. They tick along nicely in the background but never achieve anywhere near what they are capable of because they never have the right part of the brain engaged to learn. If all your focus is on managing your feelings, it won't be on the lesson content.

To the DfE children are statistics. This means that teaching small humans becomes less important than creating compliance and inputting them with data. What happens when they can't process the data, or have a memory fault or blow up. If our instinct when met by challenge to see the behaviour not the human then it is to reject it. When data input becomes our priority it's easy to see children as faulty technology rather than flawed humans, sending the problem to an engineer to be fixed is easier than fixing it ourselves. However reliance on someone else means we never learn how to fix it ourselves. It becomes 'not our job' and eventually something to be got rid of. Children are not technology! Pastoral intervention is important but it should run alongside and prop up the in class teaching of behaviour, not replace it.

So this is our chance to be a teacher. The penny dropped for me when I started to run extra curricular activities. It was like being back on that residential. I relaxed and dropped the attempted authoritarian facade. I showed my personality and my relationships got better and children relaxed. I transferred this to the classroom; behaviour improved and so did learning. I stopped being a trainer and started being a teacher. I've used this every day from that day on building strong relationships with the hardest to reach children and watched them prove people wrong.

We have a pause button. Data input is on hold. Do we want to be a trainer or a teacher? If we are rebooting anything let it be our approach. Lets teach behaviour the same way we do everything else. Let's not rush to punish mistakes but analyse them instead, let's plan together ways to do it differently next time and let's be patient if it doesn't happen right away.

WHAT DO WE SEE?

"When little people are overwhelmed by big emotions, it's our job to share our calm, not join their chaos" L.R.Knost

What do we see?

- A rulebreaker
- A behaviour choice
- A child who needs to be threatened?
- A child that needs to be punished?

- A distressed child
- Disregulated
- A child who needs to be reminded of successes?
- A child that needs to be understood?

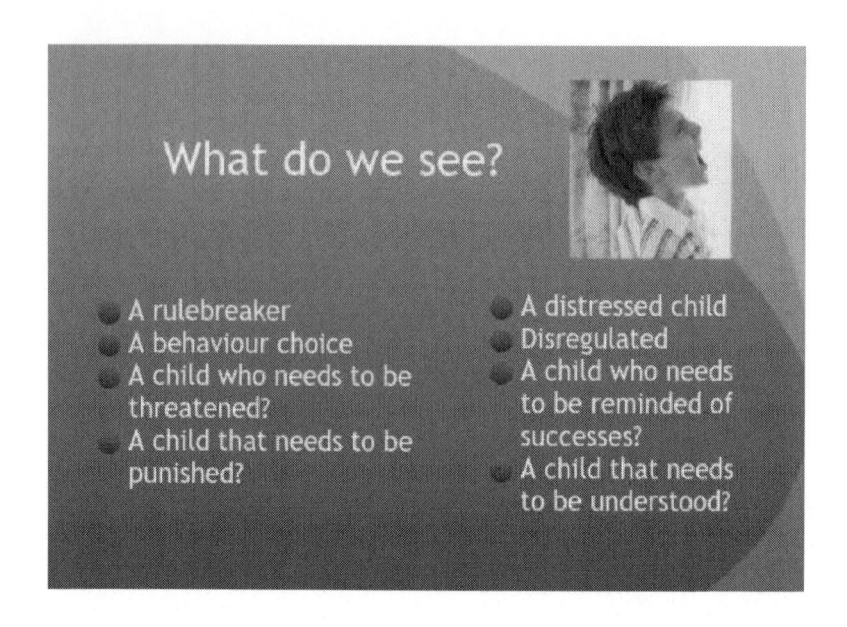

A child is struggling to follow rules, what do we see? What is our instinct?

Do we see a rule breaker who is making a conscious choice to misbehave and needs to comply? Should they be met with the authority we possess; they must be challenged, reminded of rules and threatened with consequences. If they don't stop, do they need to be punished?

Or do we see a distressed/ dysregulated child who needs to be helped?

To be met with a human response of empathy and understanding; met with calm and listened to, a recognition that the child you know isn't currently driving their behaviour because their survival instinct or amygdala is. Can they be reminded of successes rather than rules and failures?

It is our reaction that dictates how this goes not the child; controlled rule breaker or dysregulated human? Punitive or supportive? Don't get me wrong the rules are important and if a consequence is needed then so be it but timing is everything and if we want children to learn better behaviour we need a regulated child in front of us. Getting to calm should be our sole priority.

> *"When a person is drowning that is not the best time to teach them how to swim"* David Pitonyak

It doesn't matter what we say if we can't be heard. Let's make safe and teach behaviour by analysing what went wrong.

FIGHT FIRE WITH WATER

The first training I remember having an impact on me was by Rob Long in 2008. A very animated character who had a number of mantras. One I remember clearly;

He'd ask the group "What do you fight fire with?"

Everyone would shout "FIRE!"

To which he'd respond "Why?"

It's not a technique endorsed by our firefighters and would be pretty ridiculous if it was, they would use water or foam and so should we. Our objective should always be to put the fire out never to make it worse, so what we need to do when we see this child is to "fight fire with water!"

Again how often does this become the job of the Pastoral Team? Wandering the corridors with their imaginary hoses and on the end of the radio like the emergency services.

If our response when faced with challenging behaviour is to pass it on to someone else then we undermine ourselves. Don't get me wrong, there are times when children need to be out of a class but if we see that as our job done then we aren't teaching. Paul Dix refers to it as 'picking up your own tab'. If that child has gone to someone else for temporary support until you can get to talk to them or to someone they have a good relationship with so you can address the behaviour as a team then these are both sensible solutions. However if they have been sent to a member of SLT for a "rollocking" or left with the Pastoral Team to put out the fire without a resolution this is not ok. This only shows the children that you can't manage it or even worse don't care enough to invest in them.

A lot of children are going to be bringing fire with them when they return. If we don't have enough water many schools will risk burning down! If we rely on someone else to bring it the classroom may burn. We are going to need a lot of water when we return but most importantly we need to do everything we can to stop the fires from catching.

Pause for thought - who is responsible for the water in your setting?

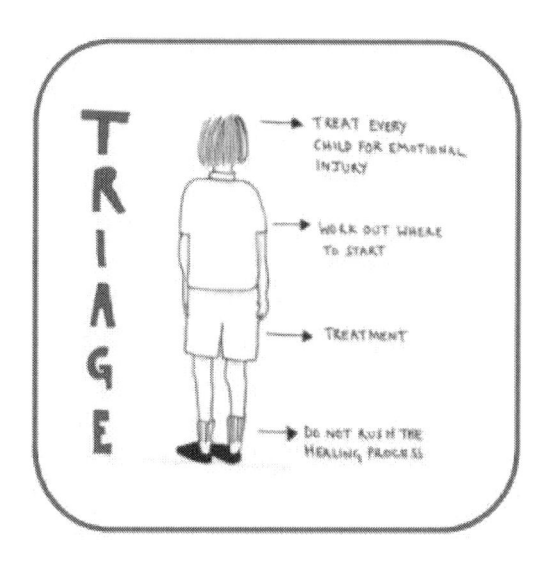

Chapter 3

Why Triage is vital

There have been times on Social Media and in Guidance that we shouldn't assume that every child has experienced loss.

I could not disagree more with this statement. Every child has lost and therefore every child should be approached as if they have suffered an emotional injury.

There are a lot of educators expressing that the most important thing is to make the environment as normal as possible and get back to lessons as soon as possible. I don't disagree with either of these things but not at the expense of having an open mind. Not at the risk of missing vital clues to a child's wellbeing being overlooked.

If a child walked out of a collapsed building with no signs of injury they would still get a medical check. It would not be assumed nothing is wrong because they 'look fine'. Carry on as normal and wait and see would be an unacceptable response. Yet we have a problem in education where we wait for the symptoms of distress to happen; we wait for the failure, then react to it. We can't get support for children until they have proved enough times they can't do something.

Ask any parent of a child with additional needs how this process has exhausted them and the damage it has done to their child's self esteem. I have been in this position both personally and professionally trying to get support for children. Arguing thresholds and challenging professionals is exhausting. Any system that only takes action if you paint a child at their worst on their worst day is a broken one!

Why are we making the people that love that child continually point out their failures over and over? Why do we make that child experience failure over and over?

The problem with failure is it becomes a habit, it becomes expected, it becomes the thing the child forecasts whenever something is expected of them. Our systems reliance on being reactive rather than proactive is the reason the self-esteem of the children I have worked with started so low. If we are truly the advocates for these children and these families then we have to do more.

Pause for thought - can we argue we didn't spot things, if we weren't really looking?

BEING PROACTIVE

We now have a chance to be proactive. We can take advantage of the pause button and get out ahead. If we treat every child returning to school as if they have an emotional injury we won't wait for them to fail.

The truth is that every child has lost. Not all in the sense of bereavement, but they will be grieving for losses non the same. Whether it's relationships with adults, structures or friendships. Schools closed for most and they were gone almost overnight. Now in comparison with a bereavement these can seem insignificant to our own adult logic and perception, but it isn't our logic and perception we are talking about. It is that of a small child or adolescent who process differently to us; they are at a different point of brain development to us. We don't get to dictate or change how they feel but we should validate it and support them to feel better.

Pause for thought - even children who have thrived in lockdown and are happy to be returning have lost, they will likely be excited but also anxious

We also won't find out what their experiences have been or the feelings they have are, unless we allocate some time to find out. We don't have to scrap the timetable to do this, there are many opportunities throughout the day. We have a habit of waiting for things to go wrong and then try to pick up the pieces but we have an opportunity to be pre-emptive. Let's Triage our returning children. Let's do our best to find out what their experiences have been during lockdown.

- Some will have suffered bereavement and feeling **sadness and grief**
- Some will have felt **unsafe** at home
- Some will be **worried** friends don't like them anymore
- Some will be **angry** at staff for abandoning them
- Some felt far safer at home than they do at school and are very **anxious** about returning
- Some are excited to be coming back but it won't be the same

That is a lot of negative emotions to ignore. If we don't anticipate these feelings there is going to be a lot of dysregulated behaviour that comes with it. Many will have a mixture which complicates even further.

WHAT ARE WE TRIAGING?

So our purpose of the triage is to find out if there is an emotional injury and estimate what it is. Some children will be easier than others. Many children will communicate through behaviour or withdraw when they have had a difficult experience so it may require some skilled listening on our part. Again we lose this opportunity if we only see the behaviour and not what it is telling us.

There are 5 areas prioritised in the sequential approach;

1. Rebuild Safety
2. Regain Trust
3. Support Re-regulation
4. Build Belonging
5. Foster Courage

By finding out as much information as possible we can have an idea of where is best to support.

At no point in my career have I ever encountered a child who didn't have a reason for their negative behaviour!

"Children don't know how to ask for what they don't know they need. Their asking comes in the form of behaviour" Bonnie Harris

Despite there being a school of thought in some parts of education that all behaviour is choice, this has not been my experience. Even what appears to be a controlled action is done to achieve something. More often than not there is something else behind that. Now more than ever we need to know what that 'something else' is.

Whatever the behaviour, the staff and pupils all benefitted once we found out what was behind it. It gave the valuable information of what to target with our interventions. If the child won't talk then start with Safety and work up. If we were too cautious in our triage then they will quickly progress through and no harm will be done. This is why the approach is pupil led. If we aren't cautious enough we won't meet need and there will be failure and probably challenging behaviour.

We would never try to teach a topic like Area to children without fundamental maths skills like knowing how to multiply. We wouldn't ask children to write an essay without first embedding fundamental reading and writing skills. Yet we go straight to expecting children to be ready to learn without these fundamental human skills in place. Similarly if there are gaps in a child's fundamental skills for English and Maths we would reteach the bits that aren't there, we wouldn't teach the full curriculum again.

We must also be prepared for children to have regressed. Many may have had a safe place at school, have built strong relationships and been making good progress on managing emotions. The rug has been pulled, they've lost their safe place and their trusted adult. For these children we may have to go back to the beginning.

As previously highlighted, there will be plenty of children who have thrived in Lockdown. All the variables, the strictness and the social difficulties of school had gone. They will likely be reluctant to return and very anxious about it. Whereas one child was sent home to an unsafe place and will likely return hypervigilant and dysregulated. A different child may have felt safe and secure and is being asked to return to somewhere they don't feel like that. They will also be hypervigilant and dysregulated. Our priority for both is to make them feel safe.

> **Pause for thought** - is triage part of your school culture?

HOW BEST TO TRIAGE

Triage is generally best done best 1 to 1, it would be dishonest of me to say otherwise and this obviously makes it more challenging in large school environments. The better the relationship the easier it is to get children to talk. The safer the child feels the more likely they are to talk. However I don't need to gather bucketloads of information on what they feel or a detailed breakdown of experiences. I just want enough to guesstimate where to start the sequential approach. Depending on my relationship, knowledge of the child and whether they are masking, this will be easier or harder to do.

School reality however means structuring or timetabling 1 to 1 conversations isn't always going to be possible. Some children may find the formality of the situation overwhelming. Great triage like conversations happen in the informal interactions we have with our children. On the yard or in the corridor, children are less likely to be guarded. There is also an opportunity to use form time and PHSE sessions. Making group discussions a safe place is an easier way to get some children sharing experiences and feelings.

Again at this point in time with no OFSTED looming and less pressure of exams, we have a choice when it comes to form group time and what is the role of the form tutor. In years gone by form groups have been like little families where the form tutor would take the role as in-school parent. Those staff that took to this created a mini form group family. As other things have become more important and form tutor time has got less and less, the vital pastoral role of form tutor has disappeared in many settings. The vital pastoral element has been replaced with catch up and booster sessions in an attempt to drive progress.

This is now a brilliant opportunity to prioritise the pastoral role of the form tutor once again. Many children survive primary school only to fail at secondary. Obviously there are many other factors but how much of a role does the amount of time spent with a consistent adult or school parent play in this? Having that one consistent person around whom they can always go too.

Pause for thought - is your setting best utilising the role of the form tutor?

If we can bring back that form tutor time it is a perfect opportunity to triage. My previous School used to have nurture time in the morning as part of form time for every pupil. It was initially intended to meet the bottom tier of Maslow's Hierarchy.

Make sure children's basic needs are met, feed them if necessary. However what we ended up with was children and staff eating breakfast together and talking to each other. The level of structure varied from class to class depending on the needs of the group but it gave the form tutor the chance to informally assess (triage) their children. Was somebody quieter than usual, was their appearance off, were they more fidgety/hyper/louder than normal. Noticing this allowed for that 1 to 1 to be saved for the most in need at that time rather than trying to work round one at a time.

When we create a culture like this children will look out for each other and they will let you know if they are worried about a peer. The 'Teach Well Alliance' led by Steve Waters, are helping schools to identify pupils to train in listening skills to support other pupils. Their 'Young Ambassadors' programme is a great initiative to support children who feel more comfortable talking to children than they do to staff. By providing selected children with a day's training on active listening skills. Obviously there is no counselling advice given by the ambassadors but by listening and reporting back to staff it is an excellent Triage opportunity and I hope many schools take advantage of it.

NEW RULES

Tutor time is also a perfect opportunity to discuss as a class what the new rules and expectations will be in a less formal and pressurised way. Children have the opportunity to discuss and the reasons can be explained. For many young children and adolescents understanding why they are in place and how they benefit them is key to them being followed. This also takes away the need for a formal assembly where they are all outlined and multiplying the potential for further dysregulation. Give the children the idea that things are being done with them rather than done to them.

Another perfect time for Triage is during PHSE sessions. We must utilise these for discussion related to the experiences of Lockdown. It will allow us to get children's thoughts and hopefully feelings which can again be used to support the triage process without the need for 1 to 1 interventions.

As mentioned, there will always be all of those little opportunities during a school day. On the yard, on corridors, even when addressing behaviour if done well are all brilliant opportunities to gain information whilst building on relationships. Many children will be wearing metaphorical masks a lot of the time to hide how they feel. These informal times often let us see behind them.

JIMMY'S INVISIBILITY CLOAK

Jimmy was the most guarded pupil I have ever met. He would never openly tell you anything about how he felt or was experiencing.

Tall for his age, a good looking lad, talented athlete and much more intelligent than he showed on paper. His goal for each day was to go unnoticed but it was impossible for him to do. He was looked to by peers and because of this asked by staff to set an example.

The problem was he didn't want either of those things and found them overwhelming which could trigger extreme reactions.

Jimmy's home was chaotic. An extremely aggressive older brother was the root of distress. Mum had made mistakes but was trying hard to rectify them, she was the parent who would fly into school at a million miles per hour screaming at whoever she could find, but she did this because she loved her child and wanted his life to be better and was terrified of her following that older brother. Everyday was a fight and that means you learn that attack is the best form of defence.

Jimmy didn't feel safe at home and worried for his and his mum's safety. Safety for Jimmy at home was in his ability to be invisible so he tried to do the same at school.

Being invisible meant not talking about home, not talking about or showing feelings and reacting extremely when in danger of showing feelings. It would get people to back off. It was very easy to only see Jimmy's behaviour. It cost us a lot of money on repairs, it got him out of situations and it stopped people seeing other feelings because they only saw anger and aggression.

Jimmy was loved by those who worked closely with him and feared by those who didn't. Those close saw kindness, empathy, good humour and a frightened little boy. His class TA would take on anybody in school to defend him even though she was often the one picking up the pieces. Those who taught him infrequently saw a withdrawn child they were scared to push, because getting it wrong would mean avoidant and aggressive.

The hard part for those who saw the real Jimmy was he had on a permanent invisibility mask designed to tell us nothing. Even though we knew his mood was generally low, we didn't know if he was managing it or becoming overwhelmed until the explosion. Normally we would have verbal or visual signs to go on but we didn't so to triage Jimmy we had to use an activity he enjoyed and that regulated him. If it was met with enthusiasm it showed us he was calm and afterwards you could get some limited conversation from him.

I could triage Jimmy by how he told me to 'do one'. If it was playful, lacking an aggressive tone, he didn't move away and said with a slight smirk we were ok, he was actually quite happy to engage with me. If it was aggressive, actually involved him moving away and with glassy eyes he needed support. Which he would be very reluctant to accept.

You won't find Jimmy in initial teacher training manuals. The process to support and triage needed so individual in nature yet if you take away his aggression Jimmy is successful in his invisibility despite all of the need for support. He's never going to tell you how he feels so start with making him feel safe.

It's what we did and the aggression reduced. He trusts some of the adults around him and is learning to regulate better. Next step for Jimmy is to be comfortable being seen. He has all the attributes to achieve in a mainstream setting, if the interventions had come before the need for invisibility, he would have.

Chapter 4

So what is the Sequential Approach?

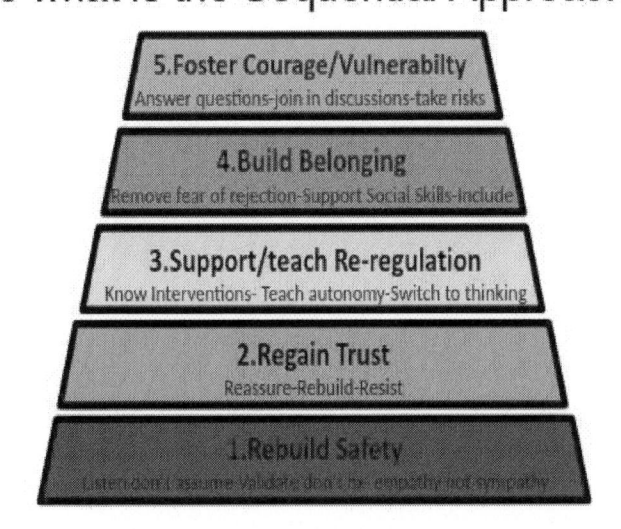

5. Foster Courage/Vulnerabilty
Answer questions-join in discussions-take risks

4. Build Belonging
Remove fear of rejection-Support Social Skills-Include

3. Support/teach Re-regulation
Know Interventions- Teach autonomy-Switch to thinking

2. Regain Trust
Reassure-Rebuild-Resist

1. Rebuild Safety
Listen-don't assume-Validate-don't fix-empathy not sympathy

My school had some fantastic practice going on; a strong focus on relationships, a multitude of skilled de-escalators and interventions, high quality social skills support as a few examples.

However for some children the ethos alone just didn't work, the work we did needed to be done in a specific order. To be successful we had to scaffold and secure each building block in turn. There will always be crossovers and it isn't that you can't do any higher stage work until lower ones are confidently achieved, it's about giving yourself the best opportunity of success with pupils that need a little extra. It's about having a consistent focus for all staff, knowing the reasons why. We are educators who want the best learning opportunities for our pupils. To achieve this let's create the best learning environments built on the strongest foundations.

Here are some real children with altered names as examples of why it didn't always work in the beginning. These children are in every school across the country.

REBUILDING SAFETY

Connor

Connor used to really frustrate staff. Every time they thought they were making progress with him he would do something extreme. He was capable of the most extreme and aggressive behaviour and said the most unpleasant things. He would often start with defiance and escalate if challenged. He would assault, threaten with weapons, destroy, spit and threaten your family. The bile that would come from that innocent freckled face would require airing long after the watershed despite him being 10 years of age.

Afterwards he would appear very remorseful, engage in restoration and make a plan for how things were

> going to be different next time. Then the next day do exactly the same thing.
>
> Staff would get frustrated and feel they were getting lip service and his remorse was fake. They would argue the restorative process is pointless because it doesn't change anything and he isn't sorry. The call for increasing sanctions and excluding would be great.
>
> The truth is Connor didn't feel safe. His home life wasn't safe so why on earth should school be? The adults he lived with didn't care about his welfare, why should the adults at school? He has to fend for himself at home, why is everybody always telling him what to do at school?
>
> We can have all the plans, all the group work, all the counselling sessions in the world but if we don't make Connor's environment feel safe it doesn't matter. The remorse is genuine, the plan is genuine and the wanting to be better is genuine but if Connor can't remember these things when the fear takes over then they won't help.

When our focus becomes safety we don't see defiance we see fear. We don't prioritise getting the work completed we prioritise making him feel safe. Once he felt safe then we could progress.

REGAINING TRUST

Molly

It took me 3 months to get Molly properly into School. She would come as far as the door, sit in reception and refuse to move. Vicious tongue, too much make-up, too much jewellery, too much phone use, a flashing beacon above her saying 'please challenge me, I'm ready to go!' As far as she was concerned sitting in reception was attending and the only reason she was doing that was to protect her mum.

I felt genuine anxiety on her part; yet at previous schools she had been told she was making it up and being difficult. The school had threatened her Mum (with whom she had a great relationship) with fines for non-attendance and Molly herself had been met with a multitude of threats and consequences. It had alienated her and it had obliterated her trust of adults in authority.

She would blow in the most spectacular style, demonising herself so nobody would look closely. She sat in that reception hoping to be challenged, she would wear inappropriate uniform or make-up in the hope of being challenged. Being challenged gave her the opportunity to 'go off' and be sent home. She'd been excluded from everywhere else, why would this place be any different?

She hated me at first. Everything about me was the thing she feared, the guy in authority who says they want to help then does the opposite. What gives me the right to demand her respect just because of my position. I have to convince this child they aren't just words.

I didn't help the hatred because I wouldn't do what she expected, I wouldn't bring any fire to fuel off. Initially it didn't matter and she'd engineer her own. She'd insult a member of office staff to get a challenging reaction from them so she could storm out, this usually did the trick. However as weeks progressed she was staying longer and being less abusive. Then one day I went to reception to meet her and she wasn't there. She was sitting in the attendance officer's room. She'd chosen a person to attempt to trust, not a teacher who is constantly telling her what she needs to do, not a senior leader who is a perceived figure of high authority and not someone who immediately gives her fire when she asks for it. Just somebody she didn't feel threatened by and listened to her.

She expected to be moved out of there but she wasn't, it became her place to go on arrival. I would join them in the mornings, sometimes our attendance officer would 'run errands' and me and Molly would talk. Between us we found out Molly's interests and gradually got her joining some sessions. There would be blips but they wouldn't be met with rejection, when she was struggling she could go back into that office for short periods and she could touch base during

> unstructured times. After time, the attendance office was replaced with my own and the need to come out of class became less.
>
> Molly didn't trust adults and why would she? They had all rejected her. It was much safer to reject first. She would walk to school replaying all the negative experiences and forecast how her day was going to go. The fire was her mask but trusted adults will always put that fire out. Initially I did have to put in a lot of time with Molly, time in the day and time with staff to get them to understand the mask. Once staff understood why she had the fire, they stopped fueling her and incidents decreased. For her knowing that there were trusted adults to go to meant she didn't need to.

If we insist on class work or work on managing outbursts or social skills with a child like Molly before the trust. It is highly likely to fail. They have to believe what you are telling them and that only happens if there is trust

TEACHING RE-REGULATION

JJ

For anyone familiar with Adverse Childhood Experiences JJ had 9 out of 10. He had come through and was now in a safe and stable home environment, he enjoyed school and had good relationships with staff. JJ struggled to manage his feelings that included anger, grief, frustration, low self-esteem and sadness to name but a few.

He would often become overwhelmed, for what appeared to other children, as no reason. Staff knowing about JJs experiences meant they were very understanding of his needs and would allow JJ to leave class to seek support. However children who didn't understand JJs experiences would perceive this as unfairness and see JJs actions as unpredictable. He would lash out, become extremely emotional and his reactions seemed disproportionate to them. This unpredictability made other children wary of JJ and made it difficult for him to belong to the group.

Our focus for JJ was to find out how to teach him to regulate himself. We could spot him struggling and he would often tell us but he didn't know what to do. After a lot of trial and error we found walking and nature really helped and so these became his main strategy. We could plan in sessions of gardening and he could

> have a place to walk if he was struggling, which we could supervise at a distance.
>
> We now had strategies for our interventions but also ways for JJ to self-regulate himself. Him feeling more in control reduced his unpredictability which helped with other children. The common interest of nature walks and gardening also helped him be calm whilst interacting with others. A Friday afternoon nature walk for the class became a regularity

The easy option is for us to be the ones always leading/directing the intervention but if we are going to teach children like JJ and Jay autonomy and help them for life they have to be able to regulate themselves.

For JJ the fear of rejection was certainly adding to the dysregulation but all the social skills support in the world wouldn't have helped. Children will never be accepted until they can control that.

BUILDING BELONGING

For others it isn't unpredictability, angry outbursts or deliberately pushing other children away that damages belonging to the group. It's the lack of understanding the social climate. How their actions make others feel, perceptions of others intentions or reactions, empathy, differentiating jokes from seriousness. At a time when everybody is likely to be more edgy than previously it's easy to get these things wrong. It's easy to perceive the emotions of others as potential rejections especially when you haven't seen them for long periods.

Gordon

Tall and thin with messy blond hair, Gordon was awkward and clumsy both physically and verbally. He found all elements of social communication difficult and he'd had huge amounts of conflict in the past which made him very hypervigilant. He perceived rejection and aggression from peers regularly and would often instigate believing he was about to become the victim. Although similar conflicts happened at home he was safe and cared for, he had good relationships with staff and regulated his emotions during class time. However he found any unstructured time unmanageable.

During Social Skills work it was clear that Gordan understood the theory, but he couldn't put it into practice. His own perceptions and ability to put himself into the shoes of others was very difficult. Initially most incidents had indeed resulted in Gordan ending up worse off. Although he would often start the argument he would end up hurt by older children and this added to his narrative of victim. On many occasions I would have to separate him for his own safety only for him to make hand gestures out of the window!

> We had to do a huge amount of restorative work that involved both parties accepting blame. He needed to be drilled on how his actions had affected others and how their reactions; even though inappropriate were because of how they had been made to feel. This also gave the other children the opportunity to see Gordan's actions also weren't deliberate and that by them lashing out it was making everybody's job harder. They stopped lashing out and we continued to drill the conversations. Gordon will always struggle but what was once a fight every break and every lunchtime and a lonely young man has progressed to a child who manages unstructured time, has a small group of friends and who even played for the football team.
>
> Every term it gets easier and he is more accepted.

The easy option and one favoured by many staff was to keep him in at breaks and lunches for his safety but this doesn't solve the problem, it hides it.

FOSTERING COURAGE

With all these children we have made them feel safe, we have built a strong relationship with them, taught them how to regulate and helped them be accepted by their peers. How do we make them believe in themselves?

Nicky

Nicky had been on a real journey from the child who used to break down, self harm and adopt the fetal position. She'd responded to the support she was given and those moments were a distant memory. The hiding child with Hermione Grainger hair that came to us now had friends and a little confidence.

With Nicky we'd repaired the damage, we'd taught her to manage her emotions and we'd got her to a point of acceptance and friendships but she was still terrified of the work. Any time that she didn't know all of the answers terrified her. She would rather not do than get things wrong because everytime she got something wrong it proved she was stupid. Even though the fear that others would think this about her was less of a concern her fixed mindset of perfectionism wasn't.

How do you convince a child like Nicky that everyone makes mistakes? How do you make her believe it's the best way to learn? For us it was by showing her. It was by unpicking all the other areas in her life where she had previously been failing, but was now succeeding and that she was doing that by learning from her mistakes. It was by using human examples of ourselves when we had failed and learned from it.

Both academically and whatever else in life we were prepared to share. Using examples of things she loves doing and had therefore persisted through failure (on this occasion it was dance). We also used her role models and pointed out the times that they overcame their initial failures.

> Nicky sat those GCSEs and went to college. She still has a way to go but has achieved plenty.

It is here we have to convince that child to believe in themselves but it's not about telling a child like Nicky. You have to show her she can be successful and you have to make her believe it. Brene Brown's talks about the fact every good thing in your life you have because you made yourself vulnerable. Without showing a child their examples where the courage to be vulnerable has helped them they will continue to play it safe in their learning.

Self-esteem isn't built in the short term by achievable targets. It's built over time with reminders of times you expected to fail but succeeded.

It's too easy with a child like Nicky to ensure that the work is easy enough to get right or only give targets that are easy to achieve but this is the opposite of creating resilience and it's failing the child to make our own lives easier.

For a child like Nicky who started the process broken, to be on the verge of being a successful adult is why I am so passionate about this model.

> **Pause for thought** - how does it feel to be a vulnerable learner in your setting?

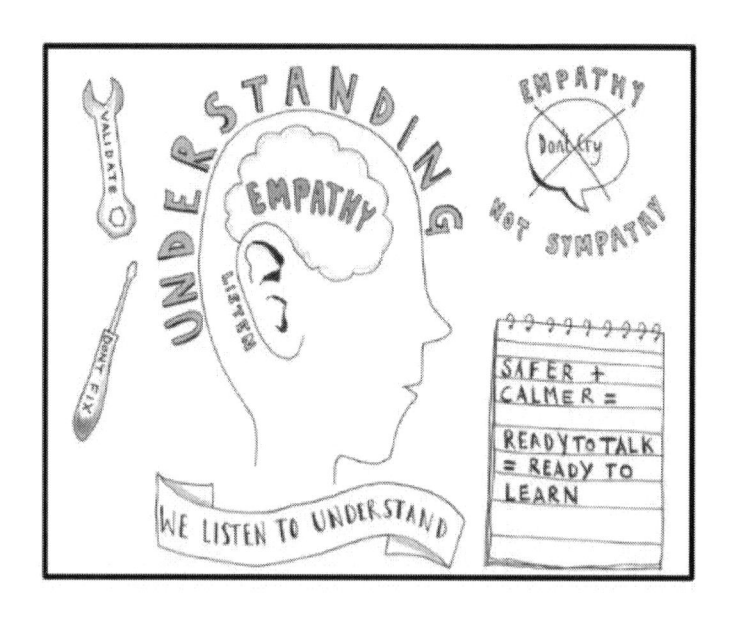

Stage 1 - Rebuild Safety

Chapter 5

WHY DOES SAFETY ALWAYS COME FIRST?

So during lockdown there was a lot of stuff that went around social media; posts that said it was ok to be a bit irrational in our behaviour, to feel restless, irritable and even be disproportionate in our reactions. We were snappy and impatient with our own children and partners, but we shouldn't have been angry or frustrated at ourselves for becoming overwhelmed in a situation which is unknown or scary. It wasn't our fault we felt that way, it was a perfectly natural response to feeling anxious and scared. It was out of our control.

<u>Pause for thought</u> - so if we shouldn't punish ourselves for feeling that way, why is it that children are so often punished for it?

THE PERCEPTION OF THREAT

Now I could spend ages talking about the brain, the Amygdala and a built in FFF response that means we can't differentiate levels of threat, but there are lots of books that will do that and go into far more detail than is necessary. When learning about the brain I've always felt from a teacher perspective I would rather know what the different parts do rather than what they are all called.

The problems in lockdown were made worse because we had no flight available, we felt trapped. With flight not being an option, it caused more fight responses. For adults this is possibly physical but more likely verbal. It is worth noting that Domestic Violence is believed to have increased by 20%. Some of your children will have been in those households.

There will have been those that are abusive and controlling who saw lockdown as an opportunity to intimidate further, but for many of those adults the domestic violence response was entirely involuntary and decided in a split second by the part of the brain that is responsible for keeping you alive. Whether we accept this lack of control from adults in a highly stressed environment as an excuse or not, is a separate discussion. However if adults are struggling with this and losing control of their behaviour that should surely mean more awareness for the children.

The physical symptoms of being uncomfortable, irritable and restless are down to chemicals released in the body preparing you for a fight. If you manage to control the urge to fight but don't use them up, they hang around, making you feel ill, lethargic and down. Over time damaging mental health and damaging relationships.

The thing is that this is not new information, but the difference is it has now affected us; the adults. Many, many practitioners and advocates have been trying to raise awareness of this in children for some time. Making the point that the Amygdala can't differentiate threats into high, medium or low. They are just threats. Children who have experienced adversity see threats everywhere, and they all feel life threatening. To us they might seem small and insignificant, but to the child they are very real and often bring a disproportionate reaction. Often these threat responses are misinterpreted as disruptive behaviour. All too often this has been met with harsh consequence without understanding what was happening in that child's body or establishing their level of control. Their brain often chooses a fight response and often a physical one.

Trapped

We at home were in a position where we couldn't get out and couldn't escape the threat. School can often make these children feel trapped, so even if they wanted a flight response there isn't one. Sometimes in a moment of misguided authority school staff take the flight option away. Keeping children in rooms and blocking exits. If a child only has fight or flight in their communication toolbox and we take flight away, we leave only one outcome.

Even if the child has a bigger toolbox, they have managed incredibly well and resisted the fight response and controlled it; they are now sat in class in an incredibly uncomfortable position. One similar to those posting on Social Media about how uncomfortable they felt. When the threat was perceived unpleasant chemicals were released, Adrenaline and Cortisol have flooded the system and are just hanging around.

So just like we were at home feeling irritable and uncomfortable because we have controlled the urge to fight, so has the child, but they must remain in class. Making it exceptionally hard to sit still and concentrate. All efforts going on trying to self-regulate and no information being retained.

This is not an effective learning environment!

Well now we; as adults understand how that process works because we have experienced it. We understand the disproportionate response to what seemed minimal threat to us. We are better placed to be empathetic to that child's needs and to support rather than punish. Introducing a new school environment with new safety expectations is vital but the way it is done is so important.

Key Questions

Will the fact we can empathise with how they feel change the focus when they return?

Will we introduce the new safety rules in a way that makes children feel reassured or in a way that makes them fearful of breaking them?

Will those rules be something done to or something done with?

Most importantly though if we think a child has managed to self-control but needs to get rid of some Adrenaline and Cortisol, we will let them and even encourage it as part of their plan. Making a child sit in uncomfortable misery when we know we can help is not only counter-productive, it is cruel.

VALIDATE DON'T FIX

There's little excuse for the adults to not be more understanding and empathetic now they know how it feels but we must not confuse this with sympathy. Children want you to listen, they want you to understand and they want you to be there. They don't want you to try and make them feel better by minimising or distracting. It's our natural instinct as nurturers to want to make the discomfort go away but we can't. We can't take a loss away, we can't make home safe or make happy.

WHAT IS IT WE NEED TO DO?

> *"Removal of threat is not the same as creating safety"* Mark Finnis

There's lots we can do to create safety. Meeting basic needs, dealing effectively with conflict, having a safe place to go and a person who will listen are all important parts. We can do all these external things but the problem is that for the child it is not just about whether the environment of school **IS** safe. It's about whether it **FEELS** safe. That room could be bomb proof, Corona proof and they could sit on a table protected by the

SAS. If they don't believe it then it will hugely impact them in school.

Our focus at stage 1 isn't just making the environment safe, it's about making the child feel safe. It requires us to see things from the child's perspective and throw away our own logic because the thought processes of a traumatised child rarely rely on logic. Perspective taking is a skill that takes years to perfect. It is incredibly difficult for children, especially adolescents to master due to brain development. However it is still an area where adults struggle to see the perspective of our vulnerable children because they have never felt that way. Accepting things that make no sense to us goes against our instincts but it's what we must do in order to see the perspective of our children, convince them that you are with them and therefore make them feel safe. Giving a child a voice is one thing, a very important thing. Making a child feel that voice is being listened to and heard is something else.

Many schools listen to the voice but we have to hear what is being said!

I will often during training sessions hand a delegate a pen and ask the question, how does this pen end in your death? Now unless they suspect John Wick is sitting at the table with them there often isn't an answer. It's ludacris and without logic and I'm yet to have a delegate answer.

If I handed that pen to a child with Traumatic experiences and asked the question, I am likely to get a different answer like I did with Julian after a significant incident.

The origin for this question came from an interaction with a young person. One that was so clear and concise a response it left me floored.

> *"Nine times out of 10, the story behind the misbehaviour won't make you angry; it will break your heart."* Annette Breaux

Julian's explanation

I think Julian could best be described as a fiery redhead. He had the hypervigilance of a meerkat coupled with the explosiveness of a Tasmanian Devil. His face is always red and his eyes always glassy. He was hugely articulate and would describe his outbursts like outer body experiences which he regularly shamed himself for.

The level of his early life abuse had never fully been disclosed but he had been told how stupid he was so many times it was a voice he heard all day long. Nothing could be further from the truth.

Following this particular outburst I'd worked hard to get him calm after flipping 3 tables and throwing a laptop at his English Teacher. It's important to note that she had asked him to write the date and he threw his pen on the floor. She picked it up and firmly told him to write the date. Fairly standard practice up and down the country. In many cases he would have been told to pick up the pen as well. It certainly didn't warrant the destruction it received.

It was an extreme reaction that is very easy to punish and he would need a consequence for his actions, but that would come later.

I asked him about what happened. He said it scared him. I put the pen on the table in front of him and asked 'What is so scary about this pen?' He explained to me with absolute fluency (although with slightly more colourful language) 'The pen means I have to write, my writing is rubbish and everyone will see, they will think I'm stupid.'

He went on 'So when we're out of class they'll make fun of me which will make me angry and I will end up fighting with them and then I'll be on my own' then he took a breath and said 'It's not safe being on my own, if I'm on my own I'll get jumped and killed'. From pen to death in under a minute.

It isn't about whether it's a real or logical threat, it's about a perceived threat. We don't create safety by making an environment secure, we create it by making it feel secure. I can't excuse Julian's behaviour, in fairness to him he didn't want me to. However I could now understand it, I could now explain it to staff and I could work on removing that fear. I was lucky on this occasion that Julian could articulate so well, many children feel this way but don't understand or don't say.

How many of us have had a child say "You don't understand?" Truth is that for all the will in the world they are probably right. We often don't know what that feels like, our logic doesn't reach the same conclusions.

Well we don't have to understand we just have to listen. We don't have to fix the feeling immediately, to begin with we just have to listen. It's also important that children aren't allowed to get away with things. Trauma or not, there are expectations and high standards of behaviour expected but it's how we plan for and respond to the inevitable behavioural mistakes that count when creating safety. We must offer that child redemption and an opportunity to repair their damage if we want to believe it can change.

Again not every child has been unsafe, the safety levels will have varied; as will the children's perceptions and not every child needs this level of intervention. However creating an environment of safety where everyone is heard certainly won't do any harm and it will certainly have a positive effect on learning.

> **Pause for thought** - how would your setting have reacted to Julian's behaviour?

PICKING UP THE PIECES

There are 2 ways to change this feeling. One is how we react to behavioural mistakes and how we move forward, the other is how to preempt and prevent them from happening in the first place;

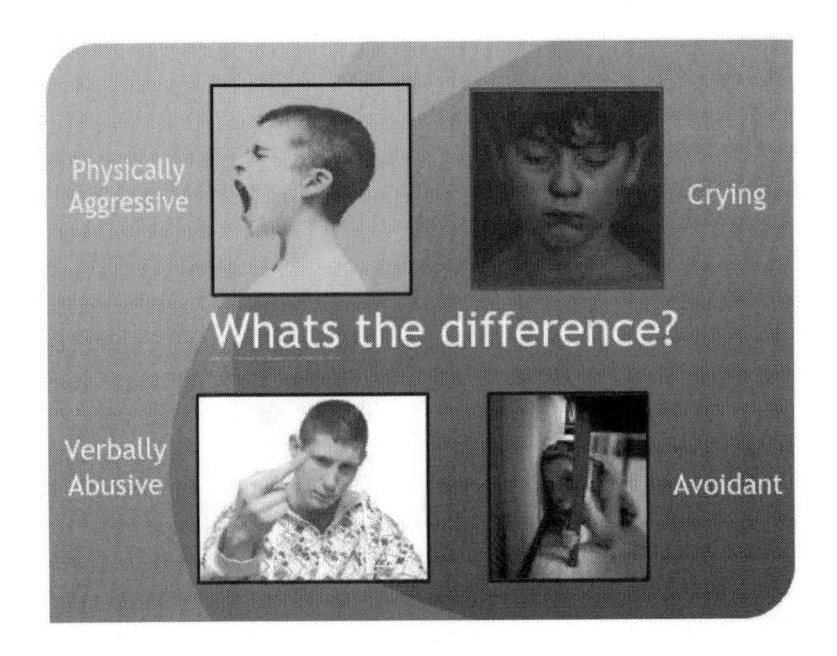

Physically Aggressive

Crying

Whats the difference?

Verbally Abusive

Avoidant

During training I often put this slide up. The question I ask my group is; what's the difference?

The answer is very little. Their brains choice of defence is the only difference. The children could easily have had the same experiences. They likely have the same negative feelings but the response to threat is involuntary, chosen by the brain in a millisecond. Messages sent to the sympathetic nervous system, body flooded with chemicals. Survive! Is the only function of that young body in that moment.

The problem if we only see the behaviour is that the experiences and feelings won't be accounted for, the behaviour will be taken at face value and the child's treatment will vary. How we respond to these behaviours is a huge part of how we create that feeling of safety. To do this, often our own instincts and logic have to be put aside.

Upset

'I can't run!', 'I can't fight!', 'I've nowhere to hide!'

When we see a child crying our instinct is to support, we see a child who is upset and overwhelmed, we often respond with an arm round the shoulder and some pastoral support, because we perceive no threat to ourselves or our authority. We talk to the child, investigate what has caused the distress, gain context and try to support.

Hiding

'I can't run!', 'I can't fight!' but I can hide.

When charged at by certain animals the safest thing to do is freeze. When you are too slow to outrun and too weak to fight the safest thing to do to survive is run and hide. It doesn't matter that this child isn't facing a wild animal. Threat is threat and survival is all the body cares about.

When a child avoids answering, refuses to work or even goes under the desk we often don't see survival. The reaction is so disproportionate we often see defiance or avoidance. Our emotion is often frustration and our instinct is to get them to conform. When this doesn't happen we feel out of control. It dysregulates us and we worry about the impression others are getting.

Often, understanding of the reason that the child has chosen to hide does not take priority over the disruption it causes, but we have to get to the bottom of why that child felt the need to run away and hide. If the priority is how it looks to others and getting them out from under the table, because if we don't it will look like we don't have control, then that is about us as adults and how we feel.

If we are focussed on our own needs, it won't make the child feel safer.

Verbally abusive

'I've nowhere to hide!', 'I can't run' but I can scare them off. Body language, tone/volume of voice, fixed eye contact. All these can be very effective tools to get people and animals to back off or overpower. So effective in fact they are used by educators to show power and induce fear and control up and down the country. Why then do we react so badly when children adopt this defensive strategy?

When we get verbal abuse from children it is a challenge. Our emotion is often outrage and instinct when challenged is to push back, to fight fire with fire. If we can remain calm, we can avoid escalating the situation but we still have a child who has been rude and disrespectful and broken school rules. The decision is what is more important in that moment; is it the message being communicated to the child being challenging or is it the message given to the other children by your response?

Do you exert your authority to show the behaviour won't be tolerated to the other children or do you recognise that the child is distressed and prioritise their needs with calmness?

In your attempt to exert authority what message are you giving the other children?

Is it one that says this behaviour won't be tolerated or one that says expressing your feelings won't be tolerated?

It's a very fine line and one very much about school culture which I will discuss later.

Why can't we show authority and be calm/supportive?

During a crisis is not the time to take on the behaviour, the brain has said fight, any threat of consequence in the moment will escalate the situation. The attempt to show authority will have the opposite effect, trying to overpower only leaves a physical fight response. Priority then has to be to calm the situation, wait and then decide if a consequence is needed later. If this can't be achieved in this moment then getting them to leave the room is sensible but it must be that staff member who revisits the incident when all is calm.

It's very easy to make a heat of the moment decision and apply an instant punishment like isolation. Many schools have such a prescriptive behaviour policy it becomes automatic but this is punishing the feelings and won't change the behaviour.

Unless we separate the two the same outcome will keep happening and what we get is an additional feeling of resentment. If we separate the feelings and the behaviour, we can bring change. We empower the child to believe they can behave differently when they feel a certain way. 'It's ok to feel this way but not behave like that' is a much more powerful message than a 'do this get that' linear behaviour response. Understanding the need for a consequence brings acceptance and a desire to change rather than resentment and further negative feelings and expectations of failure. Giving the child the opportunity to repair as a consequence rather than a meaningless punishment is how children effectively learn behaviour.

Pause for thought - do school policies need to be so prescriptive?

Is it really showing weakness to not have to push through a consequence?

If we know something wasn't deliberate do we have to avoid compassion to maintain our authority and make sure we send a deterrent to the other pupils. In my experience when a child is verbally abusive but met with calm and support they will often feel very guilty about the abuse and will want to make amends. Is it really losing face to accept an apology or reparation and move on? We will have built trust and safety in this instance which will do far more to prevent the behaviour.

If we focus on the message we are sending other children, we won't make the child feel safer.

Physical Aggression

'I've nowhere to hide!', 'I can't run', but 'I have to fight!'. It is common knowledge that animals are at their most dangerous when they are cornered. The same applies to our children. If that is how they feel their brain may well adopt a fight response.

When we are faced with physical aggression, we ourselves often get hijacked. It is very difficult to remain calm under threat and our own fight responses kick in. We do not feel in control and therefore controlling the situation is difficult. We may escalate a situation, but even if we manage it and keep ourselves safe, we instinctively reject the threat.

This child will often face exclusion for their behaviour. However, the likeliness is they had no control over those actions because they felt scared. It's also likely that one of the things they fear is rejection, so excluding compounds the very thing they are afraid of. Of course they need a consequence for their actions but exclusion won't change the behaviour.

Focussing on our own needs or the message sent to other children won't make the distressed child feel any safer.

So the difference is us!

So we are again at the mercy of our reactions and overcoming our human instincts. We see what we choose to see;

Do we see a child breaking the rules?

Do we see a child that needs to be stopped/challenged/disciplined/punished?

Do we need to show our authority to deter?

If our responses are yes then none of those see the child, only the behaviour. Our punitive responses will only add to the behaviour cycle, compound the shame and increase the fear.

It is true that other children get the deterrent message but it creates fear not trust.

Or;

Do we see a child who needs our help?

Do we see a child who needs us to listen?

Do we see a child who isn't choosing this response?

When this is our mindset we care about the child not our authority. We become trusted adults, we make it about the behaviour being bad. Not the child, not the feelings, and we start to make them feel safe. The other children still know what is acceptable behaviour but see a trustworthy human in front of them.

Behaviour is a choice but often not a conscious one. It is rarely one selected by the child to ruin a lesson or to challenge a teacher. On these occasions we have to see it for what it is, self defence.

Now we can adopt the role of firefighter and manage the response but if we are adopting the Sequential approach at stage 1 our job is to find out what they feel the need to defend against and create safety before it overwhelms and they are hijacked.

It is one thing to change our response from punitive to restorative, but we really want to be preventative

Chapter 6

HOW DO WE CREATE SAFETY?

Now under normal circumstances the way that I would make a child feel safe is through positive touch. How we meet children, every arm round the shoulder, every pat on the back all mean something and give a non verbal message that says 'I care about you'. With physical distancing it would be easy to omit this section but distancing won't be forever and when it's gone, positive touch is going to play a major role in creating safety for our pupils.

It is widely recognised that touch between an infant and their primary caregiver is absolutely vital in that child's development, understanding and feeling safe. So when a child starts school at age four, are they fully developed, understanding of the world and feeling safe enough to no longer need touch?

Oxytocin released during positive physical contact is integral to happiness and connection. Those are vital elements within the school community.

From a communication perspective there has been a lot of research to support, and I would 100% stand by the fact that it is easier to understand the emotional meaning of touch than understanding facial expression or tone of voice. Despite this, touch is still a word that makes people uneasy when referring to children. Even though it is something that can be used in so many positive contexts, it has become attached to so many negative stigmas that it is often seen as a bad and inappropriate thing that has no place in schools.

For me this is this shortsighted view; this created negativity that leads to dangerous *hands-off* policies and educators who fear and doubt themselves. Jeopardising children's safety in the short term and meaning that they leave school not understanding touch as a means of communication in the long term. Therefore encountering difficulties in their professional and personal adult lives.

POSITIVE TOUCH IS THE CORNERSTONE OF RELATIONSHIPS

On the flip side, when used correctly, it can break down barriers and allow us to see how a child is really feeling. It can be used to show a child that we are there for them or proud of them. Fortunately many schools no longer see touch as taboo or inappropriate and therefore it is used to positive effect on a daily basis. It is in fact one of the best and most positive tools in my armory – whether it be to help communicate with a child or meeting a sensory need they have; most importantly for me it is my way of saying I will keep them safe.

I have done a lot of staff training in a lot of schools on positive handling. I walk through every set of school gates expecting to be faced with the same misconceptions, stigmas and fears about the use of touch. The belief that we only use touch to restrain or to control. The problem is if we only touch children at times of crisis, if we only use it in the negative context how can it ever be associated with safety. When touch is everyday, embedded into the fabric and culture of the school it becomes nothing to fear.

TOUCH AS A COMMUNICATION TOOL FOR CHILDREN

It is a given for many that an arm around the shoulders is a show of support, a pat on the back; a form of praise, a ruffle of the hair; a playful way of saying 'I like you' or a hug to greet, nurture or comfort. These things are a given because we have experienced them. We had a 'normal' childhood and received them from adults and caregivers all our lives and we have learned what they mean.

What if a child hasn't experienced this?

What if the caregiver hasn't done any of these things?

What if that caregiver neglected these things or abused the use of touch?

What if the only person to give any care to that child is a teacher or member of support staff?

However the school says there can be no touch. How does that child learn what those things mean and not to fear them?

The simple answer is; they don't!

Touch becomes an unknown thing, and that brings with it a fear. Later in life when they go for their first job interview and are expected to shake hands, it brings with it fear and anxiety and they are immediately set up to fail. They cannot form effective relationships because they are scared by or don't understand every aspect of physical contact so shy away from it. Or worse – repeat the misuse they suffered within their own relationships..

What if that child has additional communication needs? Speech and language support is going on all over the country in schools and a huge amount of time is spent on seeing and recognising body language, hearing tone and volume of voice but nothing on how touch is used to communicate – causing children to avoid the unknown, often getting themselves into trouble.

Touch should be the cornerstone of emotional literacy because it is proven to be easier to understand than other forms of communication and can powerfully show emotions. If a child is upset and finds facial expressions difficult to read and doesn't detect a soothing tone of voice, but finds a gentle arm around the shoulder calming, then should we really be avoiding this touch? Should we continue talking when we know what is more effective?

I want physical contact between staff and their pupils. I want to see a pat on the back to say 'job well done', a holding of hands to say 'you are safe with me' and an arm around the shoulder to say 'are you ok, do you want to talk about it?' These are essential to helping children understand the meaning of touch and how it can be a positive thing.

We've lost this currently and it is going to impact our ability to make some children feel safe. The non-verbal communication will have been a lifeline for children and we must find a way to substitute it as best we can until physical distancing is no longer deemed necessary.

> **Pause for thought** - **is positive touch part of your school culture and ethos?**

TOUCH AS A COMMUNICATION TOOL FOR STAFF

Touch is also an important communication tool for staff when trying to understand the needs of children. Many children can't say how they feel or may mask it. I have been very clear about the importance of listening but children who are skilled at masking won't tell you. Often, children hide how they feel and give nothing away in body language – but the thing they cannot hide and the thing that betrays them every time is their heartbeat.

Anxious? Heart beat rises.

Frustrated? Heart beat rises

Angry? Heart beat rises

With boys, an arm around the shoulder and a subtle hand on the chest can give me the info I need to plan a course of action and prevent an escalation. It can tell me not to pursue this now I should wait until later or it can tell me I need to intervene to re-regulate this child. Of course this isn't the only non-verbal means by which we can identify negative feelings. More than ever we should be observing physical symptoms like tension, changes in breathing, red in the face and fidgeting. These are warning signs an accompanying behaviour might be coming, but the loss of touch for many during physical distancing is an important tool that we can't use.

CHILD INSTIGATING VS CHILD AVOIDING TOUCH

The first step in Bruce Perry's Neurosequential Model is to do with touch. If children have a disproportionate relationship with touch, either those avoidant or those overfamiliar then it should be something schools take the time to investigate..

Children who avoid touch do so often through fear. Their experiences of physical contact with adults are inappropriate or even abusive and they withdraw from it. It could also be that it was never there. A neglected child won't have experienced it, will fear the unknown or don't believe it's important. Some children with additional needs may also find touch difficult and we must be aware of this.

Although the critical point at which children will develop their relationship with touch is in the first 3 years some of the lockdown experiences may have been abusive, neglectful or triggering for our returning children. Children who are reluctant to instigate touch are children who under normal circumstances would be the ones I would seek to make feel safe.

Children who are over familiar with touch often crave what they haven't received. They cannot get positive touch at home so seek it out at school. Children who often want to playfight are trying to meet a need that was never met, until we find a more positive way to meet it, it won't go away. Alternatively they may have learned behaviours from home, that being forceful will benefit them and is a way to ensure dominance.

Not being over familiar with touch in this way is something that needs to be taught but it isn't as important as the child who avoids it altogether. This child will benefit more from stage 2 and 4 of the sequential approach.

The variable on this is sensory need. Some children will seek out touch to meet a sensory need, I have a child with a profound additional needs. Autism and Sensory Processing Disorder amongst them. Daniel will seek out rough play and benefits from a very deep pressure touch to meet that need. The harder the better and we often worry about bruising him he wants to be squeezed that tight. Now Daniel is an extreme example and could never have attended mainstream school but those children who rough play with other children, try to engage staff or even behave in a way that appears to seek out physical intervention; this could be a sensory need.

Others will avoid touch of any kind due to sensory overload therefore we must be aware of this as a trigger.

The exploration of Sensory needs for children who aren't in specialist settings is something that has massively improved in my time in Education. Many mainstream schools now have sensory rooms, equipment and sensory play. However they still seem to be for a specific few children. I still believe it is underestimated how many children would benefit from access to exploring sensory needs. In my old Deputy Heads room she had a mixture of sensory items, one of which was some Mermaid Cushions; the pillows with sequins on that when you stroke them, they changed colour. I could not tell you the number of children, staff and even parents who sat in that room stroking those cushions without even realising the benefits. The truth is that if we meet the sensory need, we re-focus the child and put them in a better position to learn. I will cover sensory as a regulation tool in chapter 9.

It's important for us to identify the issue with touch but then to prioritise the motive. If the child is avoiding touch because they don't feel safe we must prioritise that and intervene at Stage 1. At a time when everyone must avoid touch we are not going to have this signposted for us, when physical distancing ends there will still be existing anxieties around it.

CREATING SAFETY THROUGH TOUCH

Creating safety through touch takes time and needs to be pupil led. The best way I've personally found to do this is through meet and greet. Whether it's something special like greetings on a wall, individual handshakes or silly dances or something simple like a wave, handshake, nod with eye contact or a 'that's a lovely smile'. How we start the lesson sets the tone. By meeting them and welcoming them we make them feel wanted and at ease.

For some children, especially those who are hypervigilant and have experience of parents who display a negative variety of moods, not knowing how an adult is feeling is a dangerous thing. Therefore coming into classes without this, often the start of the lesson is spent trying to figure out how the teacher is feeling and managing their own anxiety. Concentrating on this means not concentrating on the learning. If we leave a gap in how that child thinks the teacher feels then they will fill that gap with their own prediction. If the child is used to negative responses, they will forecast negative responses and their brain will defend accordingly.

By meeting them at the door we take the variables away, it starts the lesson with a positive and reassures the pupil. Reducing the cause for concern and allowing them to focus better. Over time it also gives us a chance to see how children feel about touch, how they react when we encourage it and try to get them to instigate it. I would repeat meet and greet throughout the day whenever interacting with pupils.

REBUILDING SAFETY RESOURCES

Here are some resources around Meet and Greet ideas and positive touch and there are many more on the internet. They are created with Primary in mind but could easily be adjusted for Secondary.

Meet and Greet

Why

It's our first interaction, first impression and first chance to make pupils feel welcome, relaxed and safe. Without being shown during a greeting the pupil has no way of knowing what the teacher is feeling.

For many children this means they have to fill in the gaps. If they have negative experiences they will forecast a negative outcome. Creating anxiety, worry and fear.

By meeting and greeting pupils in a positive way we show our positive feelings which helps relax the pupils.

Which greeting will you choose?

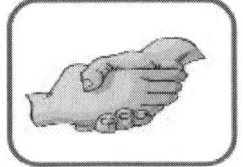

Handshake

Hug

Fist bump

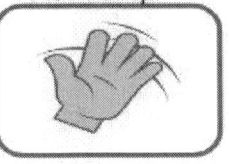

Happy Dance

Wave

Verbal Compliment

Note

The meet and greet is at its most effective when it's becomes embedded in the class/school culture. Children choose their own greetings depending on how comfortable they are because the intention is to create safety. Equally staff can adapt to what they feel comfortable with. It will also need adapting for age groups, the way a group of 15 year old are greeted would differ to group of 5 year olds although the benefits are the same

Physically Distanced Meet and Greet

Why

Following Covid 19 and physical distancing measures we will need to adapt the meet and greet. It is even more vital to make our children feel safe and positive when arriving at our class.

Even though it is the rules, even though it is for their own safety children will still crave the touch

We can adapt how we meet and greet pupils without touch but still welcoming which helps relax the pupils.

Which greeting will you choose?

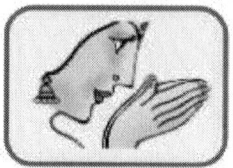

Namaste	Self Hug
Distanced Fist bump	Happy Dance
Wave	Verbal Compliment

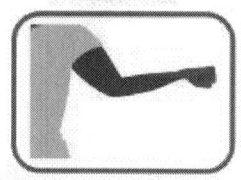

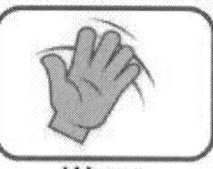

Note

Namaste - Is an alternative to hugging or shaking hands where people will bow with hands together. It is a wonderful opportunity to talk about it's use in other cultures.

Self-hug- The big benefit to the hug is the release of oxytocin which reduces stress and increases happiness. This can still be achieved through self hugging and can be mirrored by the teacher.

Distanced fist bump - the actual contact of the fist bump doesn't need to happen, could even add an explosion.

Nurturing Positive Touch

Why
For children who are reluctant to have physical contact often do so due to fear. Touch is associated with negative experiences or is something that is unknown. Touch is an important part of relationships, play and safety and for a child. To have a positive experience of school it is important that safe touch be taught.

Encouraging positive touch

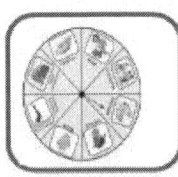

Meet and Greet roulette

For some this may need to be built up over time and how many things go on the roulette wheel is optional.
How many touch options will depend on circumstances but if working towards encouraging touch gradually reduce the non touch options.

Handshake competition

A great way to encourage positive touch is to make it fun. By getting children to design their own handshakes they can be as careful or creative as they like. It could be made into a competition with judges or just for fun. There are examples of staff having different handshakes for different pupils. The impact of this is enormous.

Peer massage

Evidence suggests peer massage benefits concentration, self-esteem and co-operation but most importantly safety. I have witnessed first hand children how children who feared touch have gradually become more comfortable with peer massage.

Games

Aimed at younger children. Clapping games, tig, pass the bomb etc all involve an element of touch that can be linked to fun. Encouraging positive touch in a controlled way and modelling play. Children go at their own speed and non touch games could be used to start

Meet and Greet Roulette

Why

Some children will always choose a greeting that avoids touch. Sometimes it is through a genuine fear and sometimes it's because it's is what they have always done.

With the roulette wheel it is hoped the fun element and curiosity overcomes that fear. There should be no pressure to do things that the child is uncomfortable with but if we can get the child to experience these things then they can see for themselves that there is nothing to fear. Hopefully they will choose touch in the future.

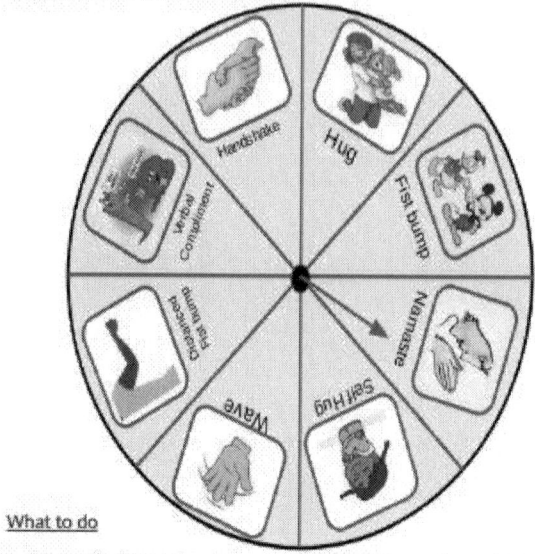

[Roulette wheel image with segments: Handshake, Hug, Fist bump, Namaste, Self Hug, Wave, Distanced Fist bump, Verbal Compliment]

What to do

Design a wheel that best suits your children. How many greetings you have on the wheel, which greetings you choose and even the possibility of adding in some extra incentives to encourage them to spin; extra 5 minutes play, choice of game, sweet etc.

Children spin the wheel and greet you however it lands. When children become more comfortable they may allow someone else to spin the wheel.

Note: It could be used for all the children entering the class but I recommend it with a targeted group to begin with. Touch can be scary, new can be scary and asking some children to overcome these fears in from of a large group could make that situation worse. Meet and Greet is also often first thing in the morning and we don't know what feelings a child is bringing into school so their should always be an opt out.

Handshake Competition

<u>Why</u>

A simple handshake can be very effective but it can also be very formal. If you watch the variety of children interact they often prefer the brotherhood style of handshake as shown below but often add bits on to personalise it to themselves. Adding in finger touches, explosions, low fives, fist bumps, chest bumps, dance moves etc. We offer the handshake at the start of a lesson for a simple and instant connection.

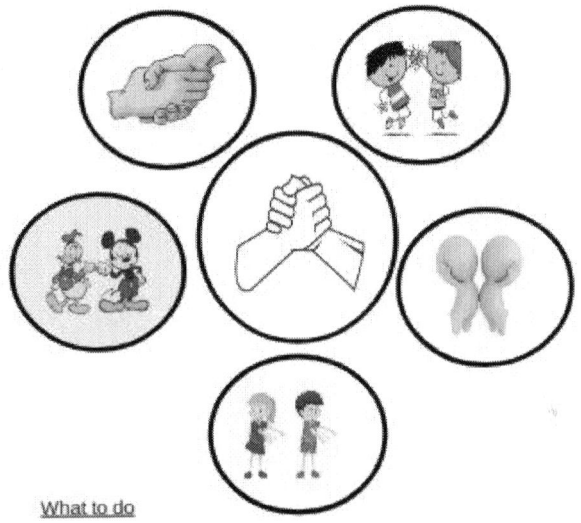

<u>What to do</u>

- Show children examples of individualised handshakes from the other schools, football celebrations, scenes from movies etc.
- Discuss all the different elements that could go into it either from the pictures or their own ideas
- Agree parameters i.e lasting 15 seconds, contains 5 different elements etc. Again this could be working with adult or other pupil.
- Practice learning it
- Perform in front of others, add music or use around school

Note: It can be as simple or as complicated as you want to make it, the important part is that they feel comfortable and safe.

Chapter 7

WORKING <u>WITH</u> CHILDREN

Touch is a vital element when it comes to repair but when it comes to building safety the most important thing we can do for children is to give them a voice, to listen to what they are telling us and to validate the feelings they have. We can only do that if we are working with them. The temptation as educators is to always be the ones in control, always in the driver's seat. If there is a problem we need to fix it or a challenge we have to deal with it. The problem is that we are going to have situations that can't be fixed and we are going to have to let the children drive whilst we take a back seat.

Anyone who has ever listened to Mark Finnis speak about restorative practice will know the passion with which he talks about the 'Four ways' Social discipline window and how it affects children in schools. If you are interested in this approach for your school I can highly recommend Mark's book, simply titled 'Restorative Practice'.

In order to help children to learn how to change their behaviour we have to support them gaining autonomy over it rather than having it enforced on them or done for them. If we want children to feel safe, it isn't enough to tell them, they need to see for themselves.

Social Discipline Window

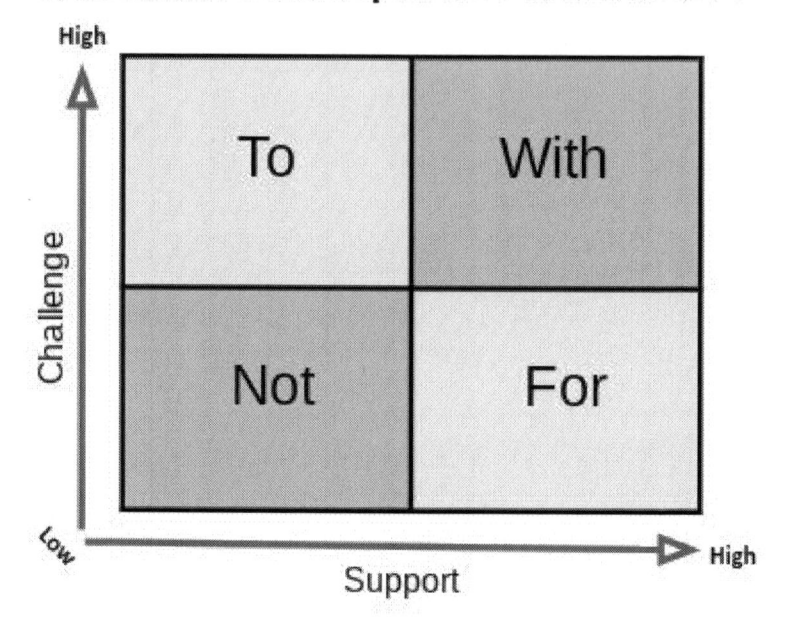

Challenge (Low → High)	To	With
	Not	For

Support (Low → High)

CHALLENGE VS SUPPORT

It's our ethos and our culture that dictate whether children thrive. There will be some children who succeed no matter what, others who fail in spectacular style and many that are somewhere in the middle.

Not box - If we are content with just some of our children succeeding, then we don't need to do very much at all. They will have the self discipline to manage themselves regardless of the low challenge and expectations placed upon them. They will also have the intelligence and ability to do this without high levels of support. However if a school has a culture of low support and low challenge then many children will struggle. Children who lack a feeling of safety need an available adult to support them, they also need structure to replace the chaos that they are trying to negotiate. Placing a child who is unsafe in the not box is guaranteeing failure.

For Box - In a culture of doing things for children we run the risk of creating learned helplessness. High support but low challenge means that not enough is expected from the child and there isn't enough drive for them to take control of their difficulties. If we spend a child's school life excusing their behaviour and solving their problems for them then what happens at the next transition? As important as academic progress is, the priority for every pupil has to be preparing them for the real world and equipping them with emotional resilience to overcome hurdles when they occur. If they have always relied on well intentioned adults to do that for them then those hurdles are going to seem too high.

I am a strong believer that every behaviour has a reason, but a wrong behaviour is still a wrong behaviour, the law is still the law regardless of those experiences. Children who lack safety absolutely need high levels of support but that support should be there to help the child grow. Trauma informed practice is not about giving children excuses, it's about giving the staff explanations. Then just because we understand it doesn't mean we should accept it without wanting to change it, and neither should the child. I've witnessed many staff with great intentions accept poor behaviour as an expectation because of the child's experiences. This doesn't help that child to learn, it doesn't help them to understand how their actions have affected others and it doesn't show them why it's important or how to repair.

Many staff are naturally very nurturing and try to fix things for the child, try to prevent the child experiencing any stressors but that isn't preparing children for the world. Stress is everywhere and we must safely expose children to it so they can learn resilience. For example it is one thing to insulate a child with ADHD from all things that may cause dys-regulation, but they need something else to support them through situations they find challenging. If we want children to develop emotional resilience we must give them high support but put them into real life challenging situations so that when the support is no longer there, they are still equipped to manage them.

As mentioned earlier I have a child with profound additional needs who is non verbal. Daniel has his own ways of communicating what he wants. He has a small selection of words but will generally take you places, point at things etc. We can usually understand what he wants because of the amount of time we spend with him. He doesn't need to talk or use PECs to communicate because we are very used to him.

Does this mean we shouldn't encourage it?

What if he is in the care of someone else who doesn't know him as well?

This is why we encourage him to ask; either through verbal or PECs. It can be really challenging getting him to do it and the easy option is to just get it but what we create is a learned helplessness and a reliance on people doing things for him. We want to equip him with the skills to communicate with everyone rather than just those closest to him.

To Box- There is a culture in some schools of sink or swim. These are the rules and expectations and you must adhere to them. Often with strict sanctions for failing to do so. High expectations are not the problem, every school should have high expectations but when they come without the necessary support and understanding there is no bridge for the child to achieve them.

Children with adverse experiences and don't feel safe aren't equipped to meet these high expectations. It is the responsibility of schools to recognise this, we have a duty of care to these children and the reasonable adjustments we would make for a physical injury should be matched for those with an emotional one. If schools made a child with a physical leg injury jump through physical hoops without assistance nobody would find this acceptable. So why is it acceptable to expect a child with an emotional injury to jump through the emotional hoops of school without assistance?

When they inevitably fail things are done to them. The list of consequences is long but none are designed to teach a better way or fix the problem. Giving a punishment for forgetting a pen doesn't help a child remember a pen, it increases anxiety and and makes them less likely to think straight and more likely to forget again. Without support the same children make the same mistakes and schools get frustrated because they never learn, but the truth is they never learn because they've never been taught.

In the to box the majority of children will be fine. They have been equipped with the skills earlier in their development to manage the environment and the resilience to cope with the high expectations and challenges thrown at them. It is a box that appears successful when those judging are accepting of a minority failing and when percentages are more important than individuals. In a target driven system like we have, we often accept that 5% drown if it means 95% swim. However, how many teachers entered the profession with the same acceptance?

With Box - Our aspiration should be all children succeeding. Some will say this isn't possible but I have never been willing to accept that. If we want every child to succeed we need them driving not their fear, we need to accept their mistakes and teach them how to fix them and we need them to understand when things are overwhelming them and how to cope. This means that they have the same high expectations as everyone else but we understand when they fall short, we don't punish them for the mistake, we teach how the actions affect others and work together to repair and we recognise feelings and how to deal with them.

WHAT DO WE DO TO SUPPORT WHEN THEY FALL BELOW EXPECTATIONS?

If you have high challenge and high expectations children will inevitably sometimes fall below. We then have the choice to lift them back up or to push them down further. In the 'Rebooting Behaviour after Lockdown' Document Tom Bennett suggested a 10 point plan for getting back to normal. Point 2 of that document said;

> *"Good behaviour must be taught, not told"*
> Tom Bennett

You will get no argument from me here, I think this is incredibly important but when it comes to behaviour, the teaching part can sometimes become muddled. We can be very guilty of just expecting children to know what to do regarding behaviour. Modelling and explaining is a small part of teaching. If that was all that was required we wouldn't have marking, feedback or corrections. To just show children expectations of behaviour and punishing when they fall short isn't teaching, it's training. If we taught academic subjects without marking or feedback we would be deemed inadequate, why is behaviour not held to the same standards.

A child is getting an Algebra question wrong, they were given a consequence then shown the same method of how to do it and told to repeat. They get it wrong a second time, they are given a harsher consequence and shown the same method and told to repeat. Is this good quality teaching? How many times would the child have to fail before we try a different method? For the case of the Algebra equation not many, but for behaviour the fail, punish, model, repeat sequence goes on and on. I have no idea why this is acceptable practice!

Effective teaching and learning of behaviour is through mistakes. It's through getting feedback and making corrections. Having a do-over to see if the changes have worked or not. No person has lived a life where they haven't made mistakes, learned from them and made better decisions. It's what we do after the mistake that is the learning opportunity. If we are truly teaching behaviour, then our children will understand the impact of their behaviour on those around them, why it needs to change and why the change benefits them and those around them.

It's for this reason we have to work **with** them. Yes we model the high expectations and yes we do something about it when they fall short of them. Help them to see how mistakes came about, give analysing feedback and show them how to correct it. Yes we want children to stay within the law and the **to box** can achieve that for most, but there's much more to life than avoiding sanctions. We should be equipping children with the skills to be successful adults and that means empowering them with the emotional resilience to stay safe and thrive.

Pause for thought - which of the four ways takes precedent in your setting?

CREATING EMOTIONAL RESILIENCE

Emotional Resilience - What we need to be happy and bounce back from disappointment

1. Emotional Regulation ⎫
2. Impulse control ⎬ Difficult for children with ADHD
3. Realistic optimism
4. Flexible thinking ⎫
5. Empathy ⎬ Difficult for children with ASD
6. Bouncebackability – Overcome obstacles
7. Reaching out- Putting themselves out there. Seizing opportunities rather than avoiding them

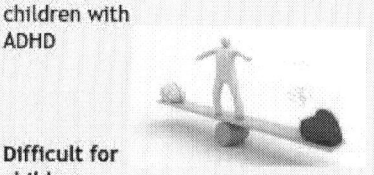

There are many different models of Emotional Resilience but these are the elements I've always used;

1. **Emotional Regulation** - This will be focussed on at Stage 3 but is a major challenge for pupils who have a significantly under-developed frontal cortex. Often due to ADHD or Traumatic experiences. They will be hypervigilant to threat and challenges as discussed earlier. Reactions are often disproportionate and it can have implications both in terms of getting into trouble but also damaging relationships.

   In the **to box** they will perceive threat and often display challenging defensive behaviours. What is behind the behaviour is not taken into account.

   The **for box** may protect them from stressors to minimise risk but not teach them how to manage emotions. Interventions take place to help keep the child regulated but they don't learn to self regulate.

   The **with box** directs them to manage emotions at times of need, but over time teaches the child to self-regulate by analysing behavioural mistakes and encouraging child led intervention.

2. **Impulse control** - Also particularly difficult for children with underdeveloped Frontal Cortex. Children find it very difficult to think before acting. Often saying or doing things on instinct that they later regret.

   In the **to box** children often aren't given time to think or their instinctive reactions are treated as misbehaviour.

This results in punitive consequences but no opportunity for repair..

In the **for box** staff understand and make allowances for any behaviours and excuse them. Little attempt is made to learn from the behaviour and repair is deemed unnecessary.

In the **with box** staff react in a calm way that gives the child time to think. The focus is on de-escalation and followed up with an analysis of what happened and a plan for avoiding it next time. If this plan fails again the process is repeated.

3. **Realistic Optimism** - As discussed earlier with the example of Molly, the expectation that children should forecast success when they have only experienced failure seems unrealistic. This is a part of emotional resilience that will come at stage 5 when all the other building blocks are in place.

    In the **to box** children will be expected to be successful both behaviourally and academically without being given self-esteem building successes. They will be reminded of expectations rather than reminded of past successes.

    In the **for box** tasks are designed to be easy to complete and the pupil is insulated or separated from potential challenges. They get used to getting everything right and expectations become unrealistic. The lack of exposure to challenge means that any form of stress then causes a negative response.

In the **with box** the pupil is reminded of previous successes rather than reminded of rules. By being guided to positive experiences where they met those high expectations, the child can predict optimistic outcomes in the future both academically and behaviourally. Once the child has experienced an equal amount of success rather than failure it becomes easier to be optimistic.

4. **Flexible Thinking** - A particular challenge for those children on the Autistic Spectrum and those with very low self-esteem. Children develop a belief system of what they are and are not good at and don't believe they can change it. When faced with a challenge they will only have plan A, if that doesn't work there isn't a plan B. Again this will be further developed at Stages 4 and 5 after self-esteem has been built up.

In the **to box** expectations will be high but the support and scaffold from staff won't be there. If the child believes they can't do something then the likliness is they won't be able to do it. They will often lack the confidence to go out of their comfort zone.

In the **for box** the child is encouraged to stay inside their comfort zone to avoid any stress. The child will be allowed to play it safe but it will have implications socially and academically.

In the **with box** the pupil is supported to try new things, the expectations are that they leave their comfort zone but the stress of doing so is supported by staff. They are encouraged to approach tasks in a number of different ways to demonstrate alternatives. The fixed mindset of I'm good at this and bad at that is challenged and new experiences are expected.

5. **Empathy** - A particular challenge for those on the Autism Spectrum but due to brain development this is a difficult skill for both young children and adolescents. Seeing things from somebody else's perspective is especially difficult for children who are concentrating on survival. Their focus is themselves and so the feelings of others are of little interest. Empathy will be developed at stage 4 of the Sequential Approach but it is worth noting that many adults find the skill of seeing things through the eyes of another difficult.

   It is worth noting that in studies done by Sarah Jayne Blakemore perspective taking was very difficult for some adults as well as children. In the context of our children, to understand the perspective of a child with experiences we have never had can be hugely challenging and could play a part in many misconceptions and misunderstandings.

   In the **to box** there will be little empathy for, or modelled to pupils, by staff. Children will be expected to follow the rules and the child's perspective or reasoning will not be important.

   In the **for box** a lot of empathy and understanding will be shown to the pupil. Any failures will be accepted but not corrected. The implications of how their actions have affected others won't be discussed, leaving a great learning opportunity missed.

In the **with box** the empathy will be shown by staff but behaviours are discussed to try to get children to see the perspectives of others and how their actions made others feel. With a lot of practice this ability can be taught. Some children may never be great at it but it is vital for good relationships.

6. **Bouncebackability-** Overcoming obstacles and failure is very difficult for children who have few positive experiences. Stage 5 talks about vulnerability and risking failure but it's also about picking yourself up from failure and trying again. If we want children to overcome their failures and obstacles we must create cultures that see mistakes as learning opportunities, not as something to be avoided at all costs.

   In the **to box** children will be punished for behavioural mistakes. Children come to see emotions as bad things that need to be suppressed because losing control of them results in consequences. .

   In the **for box** behavioural mistakes are excused and accepted. Failure isn't something to fear but it is also something to expect.

   In the **with box** the pupil is supported to use those mistakes as learning opportunities. They are taught not to blame themselves for them but how to repair the damage they do. They then celebrate successes and are reminded of them at times when they become emotionally overwhelmed.

7. **Putting themselves out there -** Vulnerability is Stage 5. None of the best things in our lives would have happened without putting ourselves out there and risking rejection. Children who fear the rejection of adults and of peers find vulnerability terrifying. We have to help to change this.

   In the **to box** children will be expected to push their learning but without the support or safety to go with it. They have learned that failure brings negative consequences so it is much easier to play safe. Children with adverse experiences often achieve lower academically than they are capable of because their concentration goes on not having an emotional failure, rather than their learning.

   In the **for box** children are rarely asked to be vulnerable. The timetable and high support is designed to keep away stressors but without controlled stress to push learning they will not achieve their potential.

   In the **with box** the pupil is made to feel safe enough to get things wrong without fear of rejection. They are taught how to do both academic and behavioural corrections. With the fear taken away they can make themselves vulnerable and get the most from school experiences.

It is clear that putting children without good emotional resilience into the **to box** is a recipe for failure. It makes school an unpleasant and unsafe place. Children come to school expecting to fail and expecting negative consequences. We can still have high expectations for these children and they are still capable of meeting them but we must put in the support. That support starts by creating safety.

Similarly when we do everything for them we don't expose them to stressors and so they get an unrealistic experience that won't continue after they leave school. Behaviourally they don't learn from experiences mistakes because the mistakes were accepted. Academically they don't achieve potential because they haven't been challenged enough and always played safe. They have developed a learned helplessness.

Neither being done **to** or having been done **for**, give these children the resilience they need to be successful. We must work **with** them. We must have high expectations but listen to what they need from us.

> **Pause for thought** - what is being done to boost emotional resilience in your setting?

GETTING THEIR VOICES HEARD

How do we give a child a voice?

How do we create an environment that makes children feel safe enough to talk?

How do we develop the skills in staff and other children to really listen?

Four years ago at School we were looking for a way to really utilise our Nurture times. We had a 40 minute session to start the day. The physical needs of the pupils were being met but the children weren't using the time to communicate as much as we wanted both to each other and the staff. This time was an important opportunity to prepare the classes for learning by getting them to communicate how they were feeling. Whether they would openly do this or whether we as staff had to be tuned in to them didn't matter. It was a valuable opportunity to triage, regulate them and make them feel safe.

We already used vertical streaming for our KS3 pupils but didn't feel it was being fully utilised. We decided to use the children's personalities and interests as a method for choosing the classes. We also took into account what helped to regulate each child and had a restructure of the classes with the intention of creating groups that could work together positively. Once we had the groups we built in what we felt were the best regulation activities for that group into the nurture to ensure that children were calm and ready to learn by the time 1st lesson came.

We had groups where the children were more vulnerable and struggled with relationships. So into their nurture time we built in communication games to help the group to co-exist more positively.

Other groups contained children who were anxious and into their nurture time we built in time for mindfulness and relaxation sessions.

Other groups had children who were hypervigilant and into their nurture we built lots of physical activity; fitness, football, boxing etc.

The crucial thing was that after these short activities everyone was regulated, could sit together, eat breakfast and talk. Within that 40 minutes in the morning all elements of the Sequential Approach could be supported but creating a place of safety, where the children had a voice was the most important thing.

COACHING CIRCLES

One school that answers the original 3 of these questions brilliantly is Carr Manor High School in Leeds. Led by Simon Flowers the school is built on listening. It uses Circles to ensure that by 9.30 every monday morning every adult and every child has been heard. From an SLT circle, to staff circles, to mixed year group pupil circles. Everyone respected, everyone equal, everyone listened to. With the motto 'Nobody feels safe when surrounded by strangers' they have created school families all across the building.

The circles take place on a Monday morning, Wednesday afternoon and Friday afternoon. This means that all pupils get a check in on Monday, Touch Base on Wednesday and check out for the week on Friday afternoon. It also gives the staff member leading the circle the opportunity to assess how each child feels. The coaching model can include information sharing like what's coming up that week or target setting, it can include personal things like things gone well, something they are looking forward to or something they are worrying about. There is also the opportunity for games and trust building activities.

The circles model creates a mini family of every year group within school where children almost have a school parent or school brothers and sisters who they can go to with worries. In turn the coaching element teaches children how to listen to each other. Every child is heard and every child is validated. Being listened to without fear of judgement creates a safe environment for pupils and a knowledge that if something goes wrong there is enough built up capital to repair it. You can see videos of the work at Carr Manor on their website.

LIVE - ACTIVE LISTENING

It is clear from this chapter that focussing solely on safety is impossible. There will inevitably be crossovers into other stages. There have been lots of ideas for how to create that environment where a child feels safe enough to talk. When we have created that the real skills of active listening are needed.

I think the following LIVE acronym sums it up and we must remember that we aren't trying to fix or apply our own logic. We are building connection through empathy and validation.

L isten - Children have to feel like it's a safe place and they have a voice

I ntuitive - work out what they are feeling

V alidate - Be Human, share feelings, accept

E mpathy - don't minimise, don't compare, just be with them

It doesn't matter what they tell us and it doesn't matter how. Even if they tell us Aliens landed and forced them to behave the way they did, it doesn't matter that it's nonsense and lies. What they are telling us pales in comparison to the fact we are listening. We can deal with what they are saying later or we may have to read between the lines. I'm sure people have listened to a distressed friend or family member who has said the most outrageous and nonsensical things because they weren't thinking clearly.

Is the instinct to correct them or just let them get it out?

We instinctively know that by letting them rant and offload we are helping them, if if we disagree we say nothing. By simply releasing it, it helps. We wouldn't challenge them at this point on the language or appropriateness of what they are saying. We may do later but this is not the time for that.

Why do we not give children the same opportunity?

Pause for thought - do children have a safe place and enough opportunity to offload what they feel?

Sometimes children give snippets of information deliberately, sometimes by accident but they rarely just tell you how they are feeling just like that. When they have had a chance to offload we have to be skilled in our questioning to find out as much information as we can. We must have the attitude that they probably don't know themselves so working together to find out also builds safety and trust.

> *"We think we listen, but very rarely do we listen with real understanding, true empathy. Yet listening, of this very special kind, is one of the most potent forces for change that I know"* Carl Rogers

I have said it before but can't emphasise it enough, **validate don't fix!**

Children don't expect the feelings taken away but they are looking for you for support. Sharing your own experiences and negative feelings creates a very human connection. We must try to see from the child's perspective which can be very difficult if we don't have shared experiences. If this is the case then acceptance is the most important thing.

> "Empathy fuels connection, sympathy drives disconnection" *Brene Brown*

Their experience and their feelings are theirs alone and nobody else's. We can't compare them to anyone elses and having feelings is never wrong.

When children don't feel judged and feel supported they will feel safe. We can move on to the next stage.

REASSURE
R
REASSURE YOU AREN'T GOING TO LEAVE AGAIN

RE-ENGAGE
R
RE-ENGAGE THE RELATIONSHIP

RESIST
R
RESIST THE CHALLENGES

Stage 2 - Regain Trust

Chapter 8

WILL YOU KEEP COMING BACK?

So we have triaged the child and we are confident they feel safe but their attitude towards the adults in school seems to be different. Or we used some activities at Stage 1 to create safety and are moving on to Stage 2. Children's initial relationships with adults in school are often determined by relationships at home. The way those adults behave will shape the expectations of how all adults behave. It's the child's experiences with adults in their past that determine their responses to adults in the present.

Our usual experiences of attachment in school are children who display different attachment related behaviours, they do so because needs haven't been met, usually in infancy, that have altered the child's perception of adults and in many cases this is related to safety. However we have already worked hard to create that, so the other thing these children will take time to have is trust.

I've lost count of the number of children who came to school without trust of adults, many of whom were adopted or in the care system, but not always. Children who are still at home but with parents who drink or take drugs, homes with single parents where the other parent comes and goes, families suffering bereavement that have struggled with grief. There are a multitude of reasons why that child might feel detached from their caregiver and that often puts school in the position of trusted adult for that child.

If that child has a home experience of adults that is one of security and care then that child will come to school expecting adults to make them feel secure and cared for.

If that child's home experience of adults is being let down and they are unpredictable then that child will come to school expecting us to be unpredictable and let them down.

It is clear that consistency is vital for these children, not just in structure and rules but in how we respond to them. Carl Rogers used the term 'unconditional positive regard' and although it can be hard sometimes, this is the biggest consistency we can give children. It doesn't mean low expectations of behaviour, it means that no matter what that child does you still like them, still care about them and will keep coming back. Your expectations won't change and you believe that they can meet them, If we can keep to this despite the children testing us and pushing them away we can achieve incredible things with the most guarded children.

> "The children who need love the most will ask in the most unloving ways" *Russel Barkley*

It seems illogical to seek connection by pushing it away but it is a natural defence to test those we care about because we believe they will let us down. I'm sure many of us have experienced testing or being tested in a relationship in the same way. Adults say the most hurtful things to test whether someone is going to leave us or stick by us. Children with attachment needs do this all the time and have more reason than many not to trust.

Here are examples of some of the different attachment experiences and behaviours present in schools up and down the country;

CODY'S HUGS

Cody was a lively character, average height but with a head and feet he hadn't yet grown into, it made him clumsy and uncoordinated but he was unphased by this. He came to our school at the beginning of year 7. He was a very bright boy who was prone to aggressive outbursts both verbal and physical. He could be extremely personal in his verbal assaults.

He had entered the care system aged 3 with his baby sister after spending his crucial first 3 years with parents who were heavy drinkers and drug takers. There were suspicions of abuse but we never had anything confirmed. Cody was now in a settled foster placement and quickly settled to school although he struggled to make relationships with other children. However he sought connection with the adults, Cody would regularly seek hugs from staff which were seen as an important part of meeting his security, but those hugs became more and more frequent and some staff started to feel uncomfortable. When staff tried to avoid the hug it would negatively impact on Cody's behaviour.

Cody's experience of growing up with parents who were often under the influence meant that sometimes his parents would be caring and loving, sometimes they would be emotionally absent and sometimes they would be abusive. Sometimes having the care and love makes up for the other stuff and so he will continue to seek it and expect all adults to be the same. Cody's

> constant hugging was his way of seeking a constant connection. A driving belief that 'I don't know when you are going to be available so I want you close by at all times so I don't miss it'.

CALEB'S WITHDRAWAL

Caleb was the hardest to reach pupil I've ever worked with. Not because he was the most violent or defiant, because he was the hardest to build a relationship with. No matter what we tried we could not get an investment from him or a relationship with him. Blonde hair, slightly distant blue eyes and a constant mischievous smile that was never at you or with you.

Caleb had been removed from Mum and Step Dad after a serious assault on his brother and he had gone to live with his Paternal Grandparents. Father was in Prison for drug offences. He didn't get to us until the end of year 9 and Caleb's brain had reached a point somewhere down the line where it had decided that his feelings were too overwhelming and so he locked them away. He appeared cold and emotionless and we found it very difficult to build a rapport with him.

Similarly at home Caleb showed his grandparents no affection and they met his basic needs but little else.

Breaking through this wall was painstaking and we ran out of time but we'd chipped away enough to get him to college.

SHOLA'S ANGER

Shola came to us at the start of year 8. A tall, imposing girl who went on to become an excellent athlete. Extreme verbal aggression and defiance had her on the verge of exclusion. She was so angry at everyone and would be very personal and unpleasant to staff.

Shola's Dad was in Prison and she was the oldest of 4 siblings. Mum would leave the care of her siblings to Shola and many relationships with potential step fathers had come and gone. Shola was resentful of her duties parenting her siblings and angry with her Mum for not being there the way she wanted. She was also angry with her Dad for not being there. Every time one of Mum's partners would go Mum would become available again but then when a new one came Shola would be dropped again.

The anger Shola had towards her caring adult was transferred to all adults. It was also safer to push all adults away because although she wanted to be loved they can't be trusted. It is better to reject people than to be let down by them. The best form of defence for Shola was attack and it was a good outlet for that anger.

> Again it was the consistency of response to Shola that stopped those attacks. To keep coming back with kindness whatever the behaviour. An expectation that she repairs the damage without the feeling she isn't wanted, got us to a point of trust with Shola and she was one of the most successful pupils I ever had the pleasure of working with. The trust she had built with the adults at school even allowed her to manage time in foster care and being separated from siblings.

All three are examples of developmental trauma caused by their primary caregiver and all examples of home circumstances causing the attachment. Each reacted differently and it shaped how they interacted with the other adults in their lives.

The problem we have in schools now is that the abrupt way schools closed to many, we have caused the detachment. It's out of our control but this isn't about our logic, this is about their perception.

WE LET THEM DOWN, NOW HOW ARE WE GOING TO FIX IT?

Nobody asked for this, nobody wanted it and nobody had any control over it. It was without question schools had to close to the majority of children and it was the right thing to do. It was the logical thing to do!

Now that's fine and easy to understand for adults who understand that logic and can see the big picture. The problem is that for many of our children; especially the vulnerable and the ones with poor communication, they don't use our logic or see the bigger picture. They see their own personal picture and in that we left them. As far as some will be concerned, they trusted us and we abandoned them, they wanted to see us every day and we rejected them and told them not to come see us.

Many teachers have done their best in extraordinary circumstances to keep in contact or provided online classes which will have helped. However, for many of our children we provide their safe place, we are their trusted adult, their primary caregiver and for many the impact of losing us is a trauma that will have damaged the relationships. In some more extreme cases we may have even sent some to an unsafe place putting them at risk and giving the belief we don't care.

In reality we may have been having daily conversations with social workers and making repeated welfare calls but they won't be aware of this.

It will not be a smooth transition back for these children who are going to display many behaviours related to negative attachment which we need to be prepared for. As already mentioned we associate attachment difficulties with parents or caregivers who are abusive or inconsistent or emotionally absent and we had filled that gap for them. Then we became the absent caregiver; through no fault of our own we have triggered or caused that attachment need.

So what should we expect;

Attention/connection-seeking

Usually because a parent has been inconsistent. Sometimes loving, other times not. A child will take what attention/connection they can get. Similar to how Cody was but probably less extreme; 'I don't know when you are going to be available so I will keep you here all the time'. Children who hang off your leg when they are little or need constant reassurance, ask countless pointless questions and want you to check every answer.

This time, rather than their adult at home, it is us that left them and we might leave them again. They will need as much of your time as they can get in case it goes away again. This is made even harder because we can't reassure them because we simply don't know. We could have a second wave, schools could close again and we could be separated again. We have to understand this child's anxiety and validate it. If we tell them it's all gone away and that we won't be going anywhere again we do them a dis-service.

Understanding and empathy of what they are feeling and working with the anxieties must take priority over academic work for this child. By knowing the root of their behaviour we can naturally regain that trust through our interactions. Seeing behaviours as connection seeking as being because of worry, rather than attention seeking and challenging we will re attune to that child.

When they believe they can trust us again the behaviours will reduce.

Withdrawn

'I showed you that I care about you and you left me!'

Trust is a huge thing for many children, especially those who have been let down by adults before. If we have taken time to build trust with a pupil before this, we must be prepared to start that relationship from scratch. There will be no picking up where we left off. If we had broken down walls before, they are back up and probably higher. The abrupt closing of schools and subsequent abandonment is proof to them that feelings are a sign of weakness and it was a mistake to show theirs. A mistake that will not be repeated!

Lockdown for this child was another rejection and the safest way to avoid rejection, is to reject first. Expect this child to push you away, to sabotage everything that starts to go well. If they avoid it at least they have something they can control.

It goes back to what Virginia Satir said and is very true of Caleb.

> *"It's better to live in the comfort of misery, than to face the misery of uncertainty"*

'It might be lonely and it might be rubbish but at least I won't be let down or hurt again!'

If we want the relationship and trust back with this child we have to face being rejected and keep coming back. We have to accept that they believe that adults can't be trusted and focus their attention on fantasies or material goods because those things give an escape and won't let them down. Rebuilding that trust must take priority over academic work for this child. If we are going to break down that wall again it has to be done one brick at a time. Not just the classroom but every interaction; on the corridor, on the yard, in the dining hall, extra curricular activity. Consistent kindness, care and positive regard to re-ignite and regain that trust.

Rejecting

'You were supposed to keep me safe but you sent me to that house!'

There will be some of your children who have only ever felt safe at school. They will feel you took that away from them and you made them unsafe. It is possible that if this child has been fully-focused on surviving all through lockdown, they will return to school on high alert and angry. There is a chance they may have been dis-regulated for long periods and the time spent to create safety and trust will have been eroded. If the child who is withdrawn has regressed in terms of trust, this child is even further back, feeling unsafe. We simply have to start again.

If we try to teach this child in a dis-regulated state they will learn nothing. Children who perceive threat cannot think about anything other than survival. Our sole focus for this child is finding ways to regulate and make them feel safe. If we do that over time, we can regain their trust and once again get them to a place where they can learn.

Others, like Shola, will feel let down and angry because of it. They may feel like you were supposed to be there but left them just like all the other adults they care about. They may aggressively reject your attempts to return to normal. Trying to control the things they can, in this case their behaviour. By rejecting you and by you accepting it, it confirms the belief that adults can't be trusted.

Therefore we can't let them accept it!

Every challenge and test that comes from this child we must pass. If a behaviour is unacceptable the behaviour gets the negativity it warrants but the child gets care. We must differentiate shame from guilt. The child must know they did a bad thing but are not a bad child. I don't like your behaviour but I really like you. When the child realises that behaviour is no longer a weapon that will impact the relationship and you will no longer be pushed away.

The behaviour no longer holds any power!

Some will say we shouldn't have to do this, some will only be interested in the behaviour and not wish to separate the guilt and shame. Some will even say that trust should be expected not earned but we can't expect children to trust us just because we are adults in positions of authority, especially when the adults in their life have shown them the opposite. We must be able to put ourselves in the shoes of the child and demonstrate empathy. If you want the child to give you their best, you can't give up on them at their worst!

<u>Pause for thought</u> - what can be done in your setting to prepare for the potential increase in attachment behaviours?

YOU HAVE TO MATTER!

Every meeting with a child builds capital. Consistent responses wherever the interactions take place is what shows the child you are caring and trustworthy. It's also where you show your humanity and where you achieve the investment. Children who struggle with trust have no interest in authority, they probably have little interest in the school. They aren't bothered by rules or by rewards or by consequences, but they might care what someone thinks. They might be bothered by what you think and not want to let you down. If they know the rules are important to you they won't want to break them, if they see your passion for a subject they might be more inclined to find out why and if they believe that you believe in them they may believe in themselves. This rarely happens in the classroom. It is the constant and consistent human interactions around school that achieve this.

TEAM TEACHING WITH DANE

I had come to understand the importance of relationships and made it central to everything I did but I didn't see the true power until my 4th year of teaching. I'd learned that a great way to build rapport with kids was to share a passion and one of mine was football. I was new to the school, I'd joined the kids for a game at break time and a pupil I didn't know came to talk to me at the end. He said I was a good player, who did I play for, who did I support etc. We had a 5 minute interaction, he told me I was sound and we went off to our lessons. Dane himself was a good footballer although he preferred Rugby. Strong and broad shouldered, he had the physique of an adult despite his 15 years. No filter, no nonsense and no impulse control.

Later that afternoon I'd been given a Yr 10 English cover lesson (this PE Teacher's worst nightmare) and I was struggling. Not only with the content but the behaviour as well.

Then in strolled Dane, more than likely out without permission. He quickly saw me struggling with my class and had every opportunity to join in with the negative behaviour, but he didn't, instead he stood alongside me, told the other children to stop messing about and helped me teach the lesson. The children in the class respected him, I had gained respect from him on the yard and therefore I had respect by association. It won't go down in History as the best lesson I'd ever taught but because of my small interaction at break time it wouldn't go down as one of my worst.

More importantly I now had capital going forward with all of these children, and just by joining in at yard.

EVERY INTERACTION COUNTS

What happened with Dane confirmed what Jamie had already shown me at university, it isn't the classroom that counts, it's everywhere else. It's every opportunity to show you are a human being not just a teacher. Build this up at every opportunity. Using things like the Coaching Circles and the meet and greet are brilliant but there are hundreds of opportunities during a school week. Get out on yard, talk to children on corridors, do extra-curricular stuff. The small investments that we make as teachers may bring huge investments from children later on. The Holy Grail of trust building is the school residential, the teacher has to be replaced by the human and that is what children are drawn to.

If we are to regain our trust that we lost from these pupils we have to cash in the capital we had built up before lockdown and work hard to create more when we return. Prioritising this is vital to getting to stage 3.

Pause for thought - what extras are you doing to build that capital with students?

BUILDING TRUST THROUGH REPAIR

Our reactions when things go wrong can often be a powerful relationship building tool. The most important thing we must demonstrate is calmness when there is chaos, but what we do after an incident can be just as vital. Just like how we react in the heat of the moment means the difference between safe or unsafe, escalation or de-escalation. What we do post incident holds the same power. When a child makes a behavioural mistake we have a decision to make.

- Do we punish and cause resentment, potentially damaging the relationship
- Do we punish and add to the child's narrative that they are bad and deserve what they get
- Do we take a restorative approach, teach the child to learn from mistakes and give them the opportunity to repair what is broken. Not only does this enhance your relationship with the pupil, but it enhances the relationship with the person who was affected by their actions and most importantly it helps their relationship with themselves. It separates the shame and the guilt

Rather than: 'I'm bad I deserve to be punished and I'll keep being bad'

Let's make it: 'I messed up, help me fix it.'

When the role of that staff member changes from punisher to helper, trust is forged.

MARTIN'S LAMP

Martin was one of our younger pupils who enjoyed school but was very selective of staff he would go to. He looked so innocent with his cheeky grin and smiley eyes. Not a second of impulse control and had to touch everything. We suspect this is curiosity and sensory seeking in equal measure but it has you flitting from wanting to cuddle him and throttle him many times per day.

We were progressing though, he was very slowly learning to regulate but was extremely impulsive and would get himself into trouble with the most random acts. Martin would visit me at least once a day in my office to say hello in his unique way, which was usually pinching something off my desk or closing down my computer.

He had many adverse experiences that impacted his social communication and his opinion of himself was that he was bad, worthless and broken, but we were starting to chip away at that.

On one particular day Martin had an altercation with another pupil in class. He reacted with flight and left the class. The first thing he found was a padlock that had been left on a wall by the site supervisor whilst he fixed a gate. In true Martin style he instinctively picked up the padlock and threw it over the fence into some bushes. He was then challenged by staff and the situation escalated with Martin being verbally abusive.

I managed to get Martin away from that situation and calm him down. We talked about what happened and how the padlock was expensive and the gate needed to be locked. The site supervisor would have to go to the shop and buy another one which meant he was going to lose time to do his other jobs. Martin immediately asked if we could go and find it.

We spent 20 minutes searching the undergrowth without finding the padlock but Martin was impressed with what he did find; although me not so much. Martin found a very old, very battered, very dirty old wall lamp. We never found the Padlock but we had the lamp. Many of the children I have worked with find saying sorry difficult and Martin was definitely one of them, I also believe forcing children to say sorry when they don't mean it is about adult control and achieves very little. I knew Martin was sorry and I knew he wanted to show it rather than say it.

Due to having to go out of school to look for the padlock it meant we had to return via the front office. Next to the front office is the school Art Garden. In that garden is the site supervisors shed. I suggested to Martin that we should refurbish the lamp and make it into a flower planter that we could put on the side of the shed as a gift. Martin was thrilled by the idea. So for half an hour each day we would get together to work on the lamp and it turned out great.

Martin was able to show he was sorry and make something good out of a failure. He could change that narrative he had about himself. What a wonderful metaphor for his own life – of something being broken, unwanted and worthless being turned it into something unique, beautiful and wanted.

Most importantly of all, Martin had to walk past that planter every morning and be reminded.

I know this is quite a time consuming project that couldn't be done for every pupil but the principles of repair don't have to be. Martin could have helped in many other ways but this process concreted our trust and the 30 minutes for a week will be paid back over and over now he knows that he isn't the narrative he's created for himself.

He will make more mistakes but learning to fix them is the perfect first step to learning to avoid them.

The time spent early on will save so much time in the future.

> **Pause for thought** - is there adequate investment in repair in your setting?

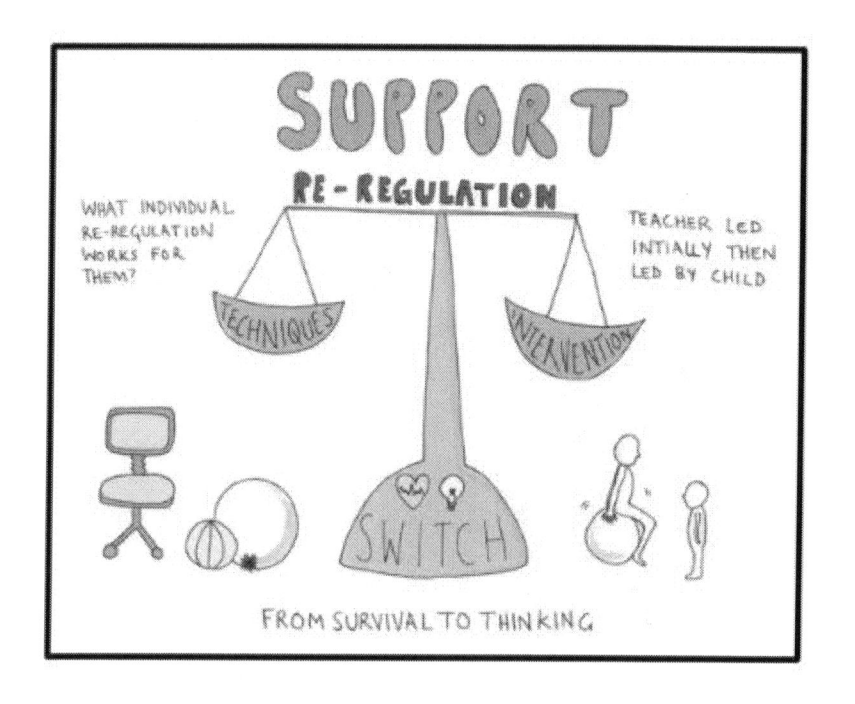

3. Teach/Support Re-Regulation

Chapter 9

Why do we need to teach self-regulation?

> *"Self-regulation can be taught to many kids who cycle between frantic activity and immobility. In addition to reading, writing and arithmetic, all kids need to learn self-awareness, self-regulation, and communication as part of their core curriculum. Just as we teach history and geography, we need to teach children how their brains and bodies work. For adults and children alike, being in control of ourselves requires becoming familiar with our inner world and accurately identifying what scares us, upsets, or delights us"* - Bessel A. van der Kolk

"They should know how to control themselves!" or *"They should have been taught by parents!"*

These are just a couple of things I repeatedly hear when referring to children having dysregulated behaviour breakdowns. It seems accepted that some children starting school haven't been taught to read and write, talk particularly well, even be able to toilet themselves, but we immediately set about and spend years teaching these skills. Yet if a child doesn't know how to self soothe we treat the missing skill differently and don't often go about teaching it in the same way.

It can be very easy to blame the child for not being able to do, the thing they've never been taught, especially with older children. This seems spectacularly unfair to me!

There are a set of skills children should be taught in infancy. Self soothing is one of them and if it hasn't been then we have to teach it. It can be argued whether that is right or wrong but if we want that child to succeed they will need this skill. When babies are distressed and cry their caregiver picks them up, the baby's fast heart rate gradually synchronises with the caregiver and the baby is soothed. This co-regulation led by the caregiver teaches the infant to self-regulate over time. If this hasn't consistently happened, the child won't have this skill.

Why is it that if the child isn't toilet trained, lacks basic literacy and numeracy skills or lacks language, we aim our frustration towards the caregiver. Yet when the child can't calm themselves down and behaves with aggression we often direct that frustration at the child?

As mentioned earlier it is because our natural instincts faced with aggression aren't to support. This instinct will change if we look behind the dysregulation.

> *"Nine times out of ten, the story behind the misbehaviour won't make you angry; it will break your heart"* -Annette Breaux

DYSREGULATION VS AGGRESSION

So even if we have rebuilt a safe environment and regained trust there are still going to be many variables in the school environment that may cause dysregulation, there is still a huge amount to be worried about that may be overwhelming. The new school environment will be very different and have different expectations. It is important that we anticipate this and recognise when they are becoming dysregulated. To do this we must have a good knowledge of what that child feels and what that feeling looks like, and we need to intervene early before we get to the point of an overwhelmed dysregulated child.

Dysregulated behaviour so often comes out as aggression and as I said earlier our natural instinct when faced with aggression is to hit back or reject. With the exception of persistent disruptive behaviour, which in itself is nearly always a mask for other things. Physical and verbal aggression make up pretty much the rest of the exclusions in the country.

The questions I would ask are;

1. How many of these excluded children were in control at the time of the aggression?
2. Was enough early intervention done to regulate the child and prevent it by school staff?
3. Has the child been equipped with the skills to self soothe and regulate themselves?

Now in my experience the answer to question one is very few. Aggression through anger is not a choice! It is a child becoming overwhelmed and reaching an extreme behaviour. This behaviour shouldn't be ignored and they need to put it right but to exclude a child for losing control of their emotions isn't right.

Unless questions 2 and 3 are yes then again exclusion should not even be considered. We haven't given this child a chance. Stage 3 will focus on ensuring that we have yes answers for these two questions.

> **Pause for thought** - does the child behaving aggressively have the skills to self soothe?

ANGER SUPPRESSION

In my opinion there are few worse terms in education than Anger Management. The reason for this is that you don't manage anger! Stress, frustration, jealousy, fear etc can all be managed but if a child has reached angry there are 2 options;

1. They can suppress it. Probably failing but if successful over a long term period causing all number of health problems, meanwhile having a severe negative impact on learning. This is often what is meant by managing anger
2. Or they can use it up. Rid the body of the built up frustrations and released chemicals. Leading to calm, concentration and better learning

We cannot believe that by a child controlling their anger in the moment that it has just gone away. Every one of us has been angry, thought something and not said it. We've wanted to hit something (or someone) but resisted. Is that it? Is it over? Or do we stew on it all day until we do something to relieve ourselves?

We know what we need to do ourselves. As adults we know what helps us. If I am sat here frustrated with a mental block or my computer is misbehaving I know I need to step away, I know I personally need to go and do some exercise to get rid of my frustrations then my head is clear to think again. If I don't do this I will get more annoyed with my computer, be snappier with those around me and inevitably not be able to concentrate enough to write anything.

THE FORGOTTEN CHILDREN

Children are in this very position up and down the country, even more likely when they all return. They don't get this opportunity to clear their heads and have to stay in class. They also see other children get in trouble for becoming overwhelmed. They develop a belief that the best way to survive is to hide what you feel and blend in. Despite having all of the built up feelings that have reached anger, safety comes from suppressing them.

Adults often play a role in this, for years society has been teaching boys for years that they shouldn't show they are hurt or upset and need to be tough for years, but this is a dangerous precedent to set. Equally we teach them anger is bad and must be managed.

We are at best not noticing what is happening to these children, and at worst ignoring them. They are being forgotten in favour of the high achievers or the high tariff pupils. They have made themselves invisible and it is easy to be complicit in this. They don't cause any bother and don't take up any vital additional resources, but if what we have shown them is children receiving heavy punishments like isolation and exclusion for becoming overwhelmed; then the message we send out is that, 'if your feelings get the better of you, you will be rejected'. The message the child gets is 'nobody cares what I feel, feelings are bad, I am bad'. When we shame children for feeling bad we are completing a cycle that is never going to allow that child to thrive.

Withdraw

We have all been in a position where we have been scared, outraged or upset but not able to express those feelings. Whether the reason is to be strong for someone else or to save face or to not inflame a situation, we have all done it at some point. We also know how exhausting and difficult it is to do.

For example when your boss is totally out of order having a go at you and you are outraged. The amount of effort that goes into self-control and stopping your feelings from overwhelming you is huge. We are angry and we want to tell them straight but we have to suppress it or we will risk being fired.

Imagine that every day, and for some children all day long; every encounter, every lesson. With the concentration required to suppress feelings, how can you possibly concentrate on the work?

Well that's just it, many children in this situation can't. Some can cope just enough to tick along unnoticed in the background but never achieving what they are capable of, never thriving and never meeting projected grades. Rather than recognise this and support them, many schools will assume that they aren't trying hard enough or they don't do enough work at home or it's their parents fault for not pushing them. This narrative has been heavily pushed in the media whilst children have been off.

It's important to acknowledge that there is a good number of pupils who have really thrived whilst at home. All of this pressure that the school environment creates, all of the need for suppression has gone away. Those children will be extremely anxious about returning to the school environment because they have got used to feeling safe at home.

> **Pause for thought**- do you have children who felt safer at home? What changes could be made to the school environment?

It is my belief that schools often create a culture of suppression which damages potential for learning. In their drive for high expectations and learning, they inadvertently create the opposite of a calm learning environment, an environment where children can't think well enough to learn effectively. Stage 5 will really focus on learning and being courageous; but putting up a hand, engaging in discussion or taking a lead aren't going to happen in a culture of suppression because if you make a mistake you will be punished, you will be shamed.

I talked earlier in the book about the dangers of perfectionism but with zero tolerance we create a narrative where there is no other way. Children will learn to avoid and play it safe because failing isn't an option. This is not an effective way to learn!

USE IT OR LOSE IT!

When we create an environment where suppressing anger is replaced by using up anger we flick a switch. We go from trying to concentrate but failing due to suppression, to using our full thinking brain, We think better, retain information better and learn better.

Why would we not want this?

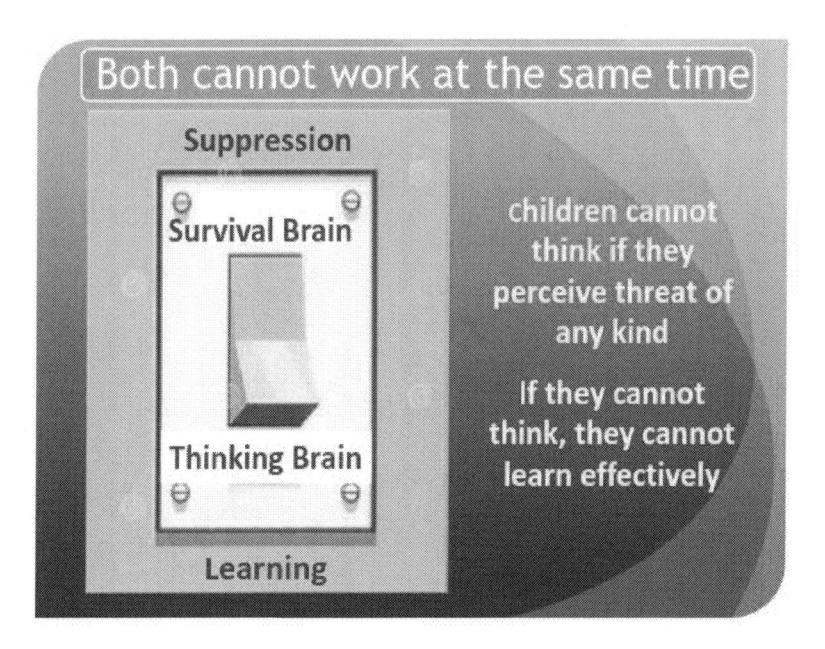

Both cannot work at the same time

Suppression

Survival Brain

Thinking Brain

Learning

children cannot think if they perceive threat of any kind

If they cannot think, they cannot learn effectively

Fizz

For years I have been doing the fizzy pop challenge. The examples of the different negative experiences the child has will vary by group; arguments with friends, getting told off, injustice, hunger, tiredness and with each experience we shake the bottle. Eventually the bottle is visibly fizzing and will explode if opened. We talk about de-escalation and not opening the bottle because we can see the fizz. Without calm adults and ignoring the fizz, some schools aren't doing enough to prevent the explosion, some schools are actively creating it.

However at least if we have the explosion we have the opportunity to repair. At least the child has used up their chemicals and isn't suppressing.

What if the child doesn't have the fizz?

What if everything is about suppressing that fizz?

What happens over time if they keep suppressing?

Where does that fizz go?

It goes inward!

It goes in a box with all the other negative feelings they are overwhelmed by; all the anger, sadness, frustration all go in the box. Unfortunately they can't differentiate so all the hope, joy, optimism and creativity go in the box, too. 'Feelings are bad, if I don't feel anything I can't feel hurt'.

Or perhaps the fizz is released later, maybe that child goes home from school and explodes.

How many parents have gone into schools to ask for help because their child is unhappy and behaving in a really challenging way at home, only to be told they are fine at school! This should be a red flag for every school up and down the country. If a parent says that a child leaves school and immediately becomes overwhelmed it is very likely it's because they are suppressing and masking at school. We have to support that pupil and that parent, not say 'well they're fine for me'.

Or what if the fizz is released in a way that is every teacher's worst nightmare. What if they can't hurt others so they'll hurt themselves. How many children in challenging environments survive all day and self-harm at home? I think the figure would be worrying.

In the moment when I ask those staff which child they would rather have, they always want the fizz. Well then let's teach children that fizz is OK and that it's OK to spill a bit sometimes. The great thing with spills is that if we clean them up quickly no harm is done. If we leave it whilst we tell them off, send them out or punish then it will leave a stain.

Pause for thought- is there a culture of listening to parents concerns in your setting?

ALL ABOARD! LAST STOP AGGRESSION

So I used to work hard at teaching emotional literacy to my pupils. I always believed that if they had a better understanding of why they were behaving the way they were behaving then it would result in less shame and more opportunities to build self-esteem. The barrier that I would come up against is that emotional literacy is very hard to learn. Especially for our children who had a wide range of communication difficulties. Add to this the fact we very rarely feel things in isolation, that some feelings are very similar to other things and when in the moment we are feeling these things, we probably aren't thinking well enough to recognise them.

One thing I did use to try to aid this process was the Aggression Train Line.

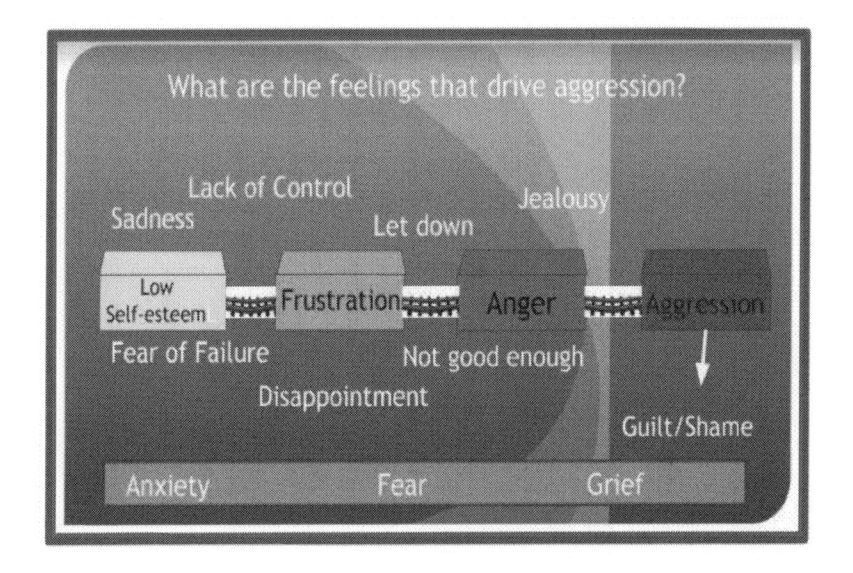

> **What are the feelings that drive aggression?**
>
> Sadness — Lack of Control — Let down — Jealousy
>
> Low Self-esteem ▮▮▮ Frustration ▮▮▮ Anger ▮▮▮ Aggression
>
> Fear of Failure — Not good enough — ↓
> Disappointment — Guilt/Shame
>
> Anxiety — Fear — Grief

Another thing Rob Long had said in that early training session was that low self-esteem leads to frustration which leads to anger. I then added aggression to that as an end destination. They became stations on a train line. It gave both me and the children a visual with a clear starting point that unchecked has a clear end point. The speed of the train will vary but it's a journey I have watched hundreds of children take. We could use it in the moment to see where they thought they were or we could analyse events to see what happened at different points and try to pinpoint the moment when they were no longer in control of their own train.

The idea for the children that there are times when someone else is driving their train or it's become a runaway is important for working with shame and for re-building that self-esteem. The outcome of aggression is still not ok but we can focus on what got us there, not the outcome. When the focus is on the process rather than the end result the child can start to identify how to maintain control or where they can regain it.

For many children it wasn't as much about identifying the emotional feelings as it was the physical symptoms that go with them. Tension, tummy ache, faster heart rate or breathing etc can all be associated with feeling and place them somewhere on the train line. The use of bottom up rather than top down is a powerful tool for children who struggle with emotional literacy.

GETTING THEM OFF THE TRAIN

Our first aim from an intervention perspective is to get them off the train. Definitely preferable to the aggression at the end of the line we can have interventions that stop the momentum.

However which station we get them off makes a huge difference;

- **Station Anger** - To get them off at anger we probably have very limited interventions. We are probably looking at a removal from class that may take time to get them out, may be disruptive to other learners and may take even longer to get them back into class. I mentioned earlier we don't manage anger so the impact on learning at this point is a very large one

- **Station Frustration** - Preferable to anger but still disruptive. The process of chemicals being released has still begun as has the runaway train. We may well have more options in relation to interventions in terms of time outs, distractions etc which will be quicker than with an angry child but it is still going to impact on learning

- **Station Low -Self Esteem-** At this point the child is still in control of the train. We have a multitude of fast interventions to get them back on track; small interactions that might distract, re-focus or big them up or reminding of successes as they start to worry about failure might take seconds of investment by us but gets them off the train before it picks up momentum

I focussed on these three feelings as my stations but there are so many other things that they might be feeling. However whatever these are they are leading to one of the stations; Jealousy might lead to anger, disappointment to frustration, sadness to low-self esteem. Whatever we identify we can work out where they are and what we need to do to get them off the train before they reach aggression.

The hope is that with teaching and practice they can get themselves off the train. In the future a hand goes up in class and 'Miss I feel really angry can I go for a walk outside', 'Sir I feel very tense can I have a time out?' or 'I feel really anxious can I go talk to ....'. Children recognising their own feelings and having strategies is them managing those feelings before anger and aggression.

Sometimes despite everybody's best efforts we can't get them off the train. How we respond is paramount. In my experience children are often devastated and disappointed in themselves. It is vital we separate guilt and shame. We need that child to feel guilty about the action, we want them to be motivated to repair it (which we must support like with Martin) and we want them to analyse what went wrong with us so we can both learn what to do next time.

What we don't want them to do is blame themselves and believe that it will keep happening. If the aggression becomes inevitable then getting them off the train becomes much harder.

There are 3 feelings I always keep separate. Instinctive anxiety and fear responses can take us anywhere on that train line at any time, fear of failure and fear of rejection are different feelings that will be discussed. The other one is grief which is extraordinarily complex, an emotion everyone processes differently and can change all the time, especially if it is linked to bereavement. We must have an extra awareness of these emotions.

CHANGING TRACKS

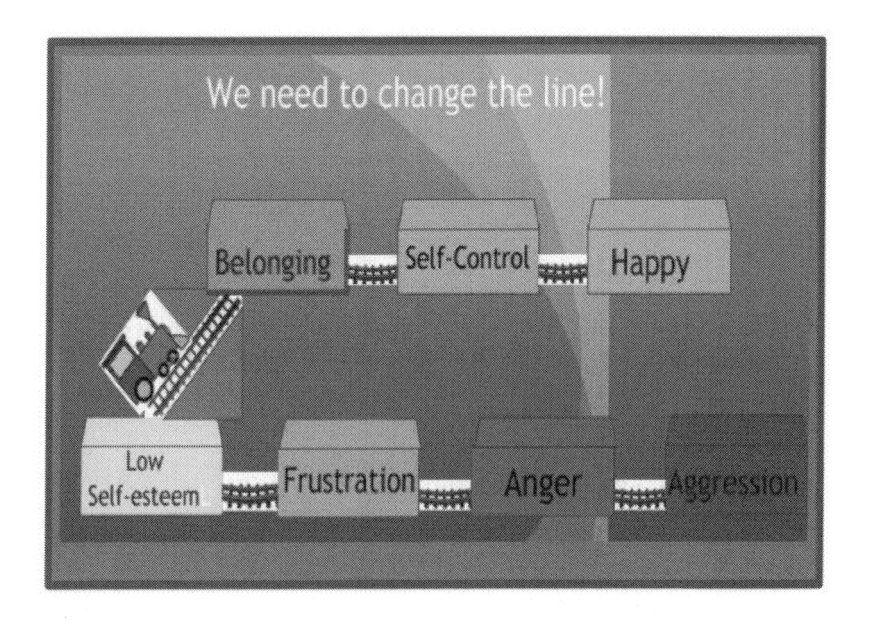

![Diagram: We need to change the line! Top track: Belonging → Self-Control → Happy. Bottom track: Low Self-esteem → Frustration → Anger → Aggression. A train is shown derailing between the two tracks.]

Even better than getting them off the train and dealing with the fallout is driving it with them or getting them driving their own train. Without support the bottom line is inevitably what will happen but it doesn't have to be a runaway train.

In all my time I've worked with a huge range of children. Those with ASD needs, ADHD, Trauma, speech and communication difficulties, sound and visual processing difficulties. Despite being incredibly different in practically every way, they all had one thing in common. From the day they arrived at school their self esteem was rock bottom. They might hide it with behaviour or mask it with fake confidence but they each started the same journey. The question for us was could we work together to switch the tracks.

Chapter 10

SUPPORTING RE-REGULATION

This train is powered by chemicals. In really simplistic terms the line to belonging and happiness is powered by Dopamine and Oxytocin. Driven by love and belonging built up over a period of time when children feel supported and nurtured. Successes and small wins release Dopamine or a small shot of happiness, Being included and cared about releases oxytocin which aids belonging. Obviously it's a lot more scientific than this and often the hormones are released in mixtures and for a range of reasons but it serves the purpose we need.

Adjacently, the line to aggression is powered by adrenaline and cortisol. Hormones designed for fight and flight which is why this train can travel very fast. Adrenaline provides an energy surge that means a classroom environment is a difficult place to contain it leaving them very uncomfortable. Cortisol increases heart rate and blood pressure which again is great for fight and flight but not a classroom and over time can have very serious health consequences.

We have to help these children before they can help themselves. Getting them off the train means slowing it down and using up its fuel. How we use up the fuel depends on the child. One thing schools often do, and they do it with the best intentions is whole class activities designed to aid regulation. 'Today class we are all going to do Mindfulness'. Now this is great, for probably a quarter of the children. Others will be indifferent towards mindfulness, and others it will have the opposite of the desired effect. This is not how re-regulation works. In a class of 30 children there could be half a dozen different interventions that are effective for different children. We must know what works for children and direct them to that. Children are individual and so is how they regulate best.

The same goes for every adult reading this book, family members, colleagues and friends can all be different. I know that if I go more than a few days without some strong exercise it starts to affect my mood, if I am in an argument I will leave and go for a walk. I use up my chemicals with exercise. My son does art to regulate himself, my other son does music and my youngest needs sensory regulation. My wife and daughter would get a friend on the phone and rant their head off (usually about me no doubt). If within a household this much variation can be present why wouldn't it be the same in school. Therefore we need variety.

I am a major advocate of the idea that we allocate a time for these regulation activities. As a tool to get children ready for learning they bring huge benefits. As long as children do the right ones. If we are going to do a re-regulation morning then we have to have a range of activities on offer. This might mean mixing classes or even year groups but would this be a bad thing?

INDIVIDUAL INTERVENTIONS

If we identify the need to get them off the train then we have to instruct them to re-regulate with a planned activity that works for them. They may initially need to be adult led but over time, the hope is that the child can regulate themselves using the skills we give.

The types of intervention will be split across 5 types

- Physical
- Sensory
- Art and Craft
- Mindfulness
- Music

Some will be more effective as calming interventions whilst others can be more planned, but each is designed to reduce cortisol and adrenaline that bring stress and raise heart rate. In turn the activities are designed to release serotonin and dopamine, increasing mood and happiness. If there has been a crisis or negative behaviour the chance to talk through feelings and plan reparations/consequences comes when the child is calm. If the intervention was planned it is good to monitor before and after the activity so that the child can see the impact.

Then some will be split into further categories to add further specificism;

Physical - Game based, high intensity and low intensity. Dependent on individual need and level of dysregulation.

I would often use combinations when working with children. If I was called to support a child who was in crisis they are flooded with adrenaline. I would often do a high intensity physical activity to use this up, followed by a low intensity activity or game where I could talk through the behaviour. Walking and talking, over a game of pool or darts were very effective. Some of the best listening I've done has been whilst bouncing a ball or whilst walking the grounds.

JOEY'S PLAN

Very powerful and with a stubbornness that would give my wife a run for her money, I used to regularly pick up a dysregulated Joey. He had great difficulty regulating his emotions and would become aggressive. When he reached any level of distress he found it incredibly difficult to process verbal information. He also had great difficulty managing conflict.

Intervention

When I would be called to support Joey my sole focus was to get him away from whatever was triggering him and get him calm. I had no thinking brain to work with until I had done this. We were lucky to have a gym area at the front of school and I would simply say 'Gym' to Joey. Most of the time depending on where his train was would come with me. Once there he would then follow a similar process. He would go 100mph at the punch bag until he couldn't breathe. From there I could set him a challenge like rowing 1000m or 15 pull ups.

By now he was regulated enough to engage in conversation whilst doing some lighter exercise. Joey didn't have the emotional literacy skills to explain his feelings but he could describe tension, a really fast heart beat and the point at which he couldn't remember what happened next.

Plan

Very often Joey's difficulties would be right after break times. He found the social side difficult and this often resulted in conflict. This not being resolved meant that a dysregulated Joey would return to class who was not 'ready to learn'. His thinking brain was turned off and his survival brain turned on.

Rather than waiting for this to happen and the reactive crisis intervention used by me. We would factor in a 5 minute period after break and lunch where Joey could do some low intensity physical activity whilst unpicking any conflicts that had happened. This shorter intervention meant Joey was ready for learning much quicker. This intervention then became part of his morning routine in a small group of children with similar needs.

Sensory - Touch based activities, light/sound/smell activities and physical sensory activities.

It is a common belief that sensory support is something that children with Severe Learning Difficulties should have. Every SLD setting will have a wide variety of sensory equipment to support their pupils. I'm really pleased to have seen a big shift in this over the last decade. There are a great many children with behavioural needs who thrive from sensory support and many in mainstream too. Something I often enquire about when providing mainstream outreach support is what sensory things the school offers.

LEO'S TAPPING

Leo was like a coiled spring. The slightest thing could prompt a reaction. He was small and wiry and always ready. Ready to fight or to fly. I would commonly ask him why he had done something and he had no idea. He was always in the moment, always assessing and always ready. Despite this he coped well and was extremely intelligent.

Leo had a huge amount of trauma in his early development but was in a very caring foster placement. He would lash out verbally, physically and sometimes run out. We initially used physical activity as a regulation tool as he was a very keen footballer but his need to win sometimes caused further stress.

> He responded well to sensory toys and used a wobble cushion when he sat but the breakthrough came when we introduced Leo to tapping. Initially it was teacher led as part of a social skills group. The tapping helped to regulate him and the positive messages he would repeat to himself raised his self worth. It became a planned intervention once a day but more pleasingly would be when he would ask to leave class to go somewhere quiet to tap by himself.

For more information about tapping I recommend 'Gorilla Thumps and Bear Hugs' by Alex Ortner. Or watch his YouTube video https://youtu.be/s99M8eJV4sk.

Art and Craft - Drawing, colouring, painting and modelling

There are a great number of children who struggle to regulate who are hugely creative. Often those creative activities can be used to release the cortisol. As a calming activity art is very effective but it has further benefits in that many children who can't verbally express how they feel can do so through art. Some of the children I have worked with produced some very dark and concerning pieces of art but by getting those thoughts out of their head and onto paper it made them feel better. It also communicated with us how they were feeling.

KARIM'S SKETCHBOOK

Small for his age, black hair and an even blacker mood. Karim displayed very high anxiety and was a school refuser. I had worked hard to get him back into school with little success. He would get overwhelmed and go into freeze when he got close to school. Whilst working on a reintegration plan and working off site with Karim we focussed on creative activities and he developed a huge passion for art. He started carrying a sketchbook with him wherever he went and when he felt anxious would draw. We allowed the sketchbook to come to school with Karim and his first session everyday was an art session. We built from half days to full days with a similar art session after lunch. He was confident enough to join whichever class and draw quietly in the background.

The sketchbook also played a role throughout the day. If he completed work he could draw or if he needed a time out he could have one. This allowed him to consistently regulate himself throughout the day. Karim went from 17% attendance to 78% attendance and left with enough qualifications to get to college. Including an A in art.

Mindfulness - Breathing, visualisation, senses and/or physical sensations

For many children who are constantly hypervigilant and managing lots of sensory input, the chance to be calm, quiet and reduce that input can really benefit. Teacher led visualisation and breathing activities are excellent stress relief for many children. Textures, blankets, aromatherapy and lighting can all help. Small group sessions would often be done during nurture time to get children calm and ready to learn

However the technique can also be done individually using breathing exercises and the senses. Often children will seek out a quiet place to regulate themselves.

BOBBY'S RELAXATION

Bobby wore his heart on his sleeve. He made no attempt to hide his mood and would be fidgety and push people away when low in mood and dysregulated. He had a complicated relationship with mum following a series of abusive partners. He entered the care system and was very angry. Bobby also had significant ADHD which meant his mind was never still and he was nearly always in a heightened state. He found managing a learning environment very difficult and found managing his emotions impossible.

One day Bobby came into the deputies office extremely agitated. The room had just been used for a mindfulness session so blankets were laid out, essential oils were burning and crashing waves were playing. It had nearly prompted me to leave because I find that atmosphere anything but calming. Despite how wildly he had entered the room he lay down on a

> blanket and listened to the music. I dimmed the lights and he promptly fell asleep.
>
> Bobby had a relaxation session most mornings after that and it had a huge impact on his learning. Teacher led visualisation activities will have him so calm he will often fall asleep but the anger and frustration temporarily go away. Bobby now uses the 5,4,3,2,1 senses technique to help regulate himself.

Music - Playing, listening, singing and/or writing

In a similar manner to art the opportunity to be creative can bring a calm that nothing else can. It can take those negative emotions and chemicals and transform them into something else. Whether using the music to re-regulate at a time of crisis or as a planned intervention it was something of great power.

We as adults listen to music that reflects our mood; whether it's some rock music when we are annoyed or classical to help us relax or the song we play over and over when we are dealing with sadness. I remember a friend at university who played 'half the world away' by Oasis for 2 weeks straight whilst he processed a breakup. We all hear a song and are transported back to a time or place, good or bad music connects us emotionally. So equally, if music can reflect a mood, it can also change it. Just like hearing a song can hit it with an instant sadness like a punch in the gut, listening to something associated with positive memories can calm us and bring us up. This can be difficult if the child doesn't have many positive memories.

Just like the art work could be quite dark at times so could the music. We had a group who used to write music and some of the lyrics could be concerning, but again I believe it is better out of the mind and onto the paper. So many artists talk about music being their saviour and outlet for their negative emotions. We saw this first hand.

The other thing about music is it drives connection. Sharing songs, styles and artists can be a way in with the most challenging pupils. It's too easy for us fuddy duddy uncool teachers to dismiss the children's music choices in the ways our teachers probably did ours, but for a child who is passionate about music, asking them about their music might be the one time they let that guard down.

CORY'S ESCAPE

Cory was one so angry it almost consumed him. Recently in care, given up on by his Dad and repeatedly let down by Mum. He had significant ADHD needs and struggled academically and socially. He would mask really effectively and behave in the way of the class clown to get attention from peers in the hope it would make him friends and distract from what he was feeling. He would escalate his behaviour quickly and show high levels of aggression.

School was a very difficult place, but put a piano in front of that child and he would disappear. All the anger, all the rage, all the frustration. You could watch it hear it leave as the piano played.

If I could get to him in time when we were close to crisis he would slam himself down into that piano chair and hammer those keys as if they had personally offended him. The music would be fast and deep and clumsy. Then it would change, a wider range of notes with less force until he was playing beautifully. Cory couldn't read music despite writing his own. He just played what he felt at the time and it was clear that his anger changed at that piano.

We had a keyboard in the class for him to play at the start of the day and built in extra sessions of music during the week. He would play piano and guitar, write lyrics and even sing. There was so much happening in Cory's life outside school but music was his saviour and it would be used to regulate him repeatedly throughout each day so we could get some learning done.

ESKAPE

On Fridays a group of children who all loved music would go and do a session with professional music producers. Children you would never put together, from 4 different year groups. Corey suffered trauma and in the care system in his 3rd placement in the last 6 months, Ethan with significant ASD needs, Nicky with dyslexia and a void of self esteem and Meena who had suffered relentless bullying at her previous school. They all came together to collaborate on a song that they wrote themselves, arranged themselves and performed themselves with a little help from Tom on my pastoral team.

They called the group Eskape because that is what music was for them and Ks are cooler than Cs, they called the song 'Stronger' because that's what music made them.

You can find the song at https://youtu.be/yaq0mzwfwGw

RE-REGULATION RESOURCES

The next 9 pages are resource card ideas related to regulating children. Initially designed to be adult led activities, elements can then become built in pupil strategies later on.

I also recommend looking at the work done by family action in Lincolnshire on their 'Toolkit for Regulation'. Nowhere in the country has done more to turn around and prevent exclusions than Lincolnshire.

Activity 3.1
Ready to Learn Mornings

Why

Children enter the building having experienced many different things, which have resulted in many different feelings. If children are entering classrooms at varying levels of dysregulation it will mean varying levels of behaviour and concentration. By getting everyone calm we maximise the learning environment and the children's abilities retain information.

What to do

- One or more staff led activities;
  Physical activity - individual and/or team
  Mindfulness activity - breathing/visualising/peer massage
  Sensory activity - physical/textures/pressure/toys
  Art activity - drawing/painting/modelling
  Music activity - playing/listening/singing/writing
  Talking activity - games/circles/discussion
- Pupils choose or are guided by staff
- Children to note down, talk about how they feel or even measure heart rate at the beginning of session. Then again at the end.
- Discuss changes

Note: By children seeing the benefit the hope is they use the activity as a self-regulation tool in the future

Activity 3.2
Re-Regulation using Physical Activity

Why

Children who are scared or stressed may have excessive amounts of Adrenaline and Cortisol in their system. The energy surge and increased HR may be best used up by physical activity. The type of physical activity may vary dependent on pupil; some may favour intense or leisurely activity, some may prefer an individual or group activity. Meeting the needs of the individual pupil is priority

What to do

- Choose a physical activity. In moments of distress the child may choose. If more structured or a group then the adult choose. Often it is good for the adult to choose an activity they are comfortable with or passionate about.
- For planned session children to note down, talk about how they feel or even measure heart rate at beginning of session. When rested repeat again at the end.
- Discuss changes
- If distressed pupil let them use up as much energy as possible then talk about what led to the dysregulation.

Note: By doing this activity you are not rewarding bad behaviour. It is designed to get the child calm so that the behaviour can be discussed. If a sanction or reparation is needed it should take place after regulated

Activity 3.2.1
Physical Activity - Game

Benefits

- Physical element of the activity uses up negative chemicals
- These are replaced by dopamine
- Co-regulation by peer or staff member
- Competitive/fun element to distract from trigger
- Easy to bring in communication for post incident learning

What to do

- Staff/pupil, pupil/pupil or small group
- For planned session children to note down, talk about how they feel or even measure heart rate at beginning of session. When rested repeat again at the end.
- Discuss changes in how they feel
- Discuss the incident of dysregulation, link to feeling and make a plan for self-regulation
- Decide consequence and/or reparation if necessary

Note: If child isn't ready to compete with others and losing might escalate, set them an individual focus. I.e score 5 baskets or do 10 keep ups

Activity 3.2.2
Physical Activity - High Intensity

Benefits
- Intensive Physical element quickly mimics fight/flight and uses up negative chemicals and excess energy
- Releases dopamine to improve mood
- Distract from trigger
- Easy to bring in communication for post incident learning

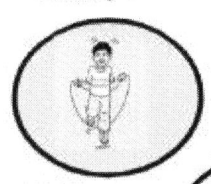

High Intensity Activity

What to do

- Individual or small group. Design circuits led by staff or pupil led
- For planned session children to note down, talk about how they feel or even measure heart rate at beginning of session. When rested repeat again at the end.
- Discuss changes in how they feel
- Discuss the incident of dysregulation, link to feeling and make a plan for self-regulation
- Decide consequence and/or reparation if necessary

Note: Set children challenges if they need a focus. I.e 20 push ups, cycle this far in a minute.

Activity 3.2.3
Physical Activity - Low Intensity

Benefits

- Less intense physical element allows for more communication during intervention if wanted this can release oxytocin to aid belonging
- Releases seratonin to improve.
- Distract from trigger
- Likely to be a planned intervention to allow for better learning

Fishing

Pool

Low Intensity Activity

Martial Arts

Darts

Nature Walk

What to do

- Individual or small group.
- For planned session children to note down, talk about how they feel or even measure heart rate at beginning of session. When rested repeat again at the end.
- Discuss changes in how they feel

Note: These activities are a perfect chance for relationship building and creating belonging as well as regulation

Activity 3.3
Re-Regulation using Art and Craft

Why

Children who are scared or stressed may have excessive amounts of Adrenaline and Cortisol in their system. This may be calmed and used up by a creative activity. The type of Art activity may vary dependent on pupil; some may favour detailed drawing/colouring that requires concentration, painting with strong colours and varying brush strokes/styles, while others might use their hands to make something either through modelling or craft. Meeting the needs of the individual pupil is priority

Arts and Crafts Activity

What to do

- Choose an Art or Craft activity. Often it is good for the adult to choose an activity they are comfortable with or passionate about. However it may be more effective in moments of crisis to provide materials and be led by the pupil.
- For planned session children to note down, talk about how they feel or even measure heart rate at beginning of session. When rested repeat again at the end.
- Discuss changes in mood after activity.
- It's important that this does not become a lesson. Children must have the opportunity to release what they are feeling. This may be in the form of some upsetting drawings. It is important to talk about those later but more important to get the child regulated first.

Note: By doing this activity you are not rewarding bad behaviour. It is designed to get the child calm so that the behaviour can be discussed. If a sanction or reparation is needed it should take place after regulated

Activity 3.4
Sensory Re-Regulation

<u>Why</u>

Children who are scared or stressed may have excessive amounts of Adrenaline and Cortisol in their system. They may also be overwhelmed by the input around them.

This may be calmed and used up by a sensory activity. The type of sensory activity may vary dependent on pupil; some may favour touch base sensory like textures, pressure changes or sensory toys. Others may prefer sight and sound based sensory changes like quiet spaces or changes to lighting. Others may benefit from a physical sensory movement, tapping or massage. It is vital to meet the individual need of the child and it may be worthwhile seeking a sensory profile

<u>What to do</u>

- Either choose a type sensory activity or provide sensory materials and be led by the pupil.
- For planned session children to note down, talk about how they feel or even measure heart rate at beginning of session. When rested repeat again at the end.
- Discuss changes in mood after activity.
- The adult may guide children but ultimately It's important for children to experiment with different sensory inputs and combinations.

Note: By doing this activity you are not rewarding bad behaviour. It is designed to get the child calm so that the behaviour can be discussed. If a sanction or reparation is needed it should take place after regulated

Activity 3.4.1
Sensory Activity - Touch

Aims

- Help to calm anxiety and meet sensory need
- Help concentration and focus
- Distract from trigger
- Help child to talk

Toys

Tapping

Sensory touch Activity

Sand/water

Weighted Blanket

Textures

Activities

- Wide range of sensory toys I.e spinners, egg timers, fidget toys designed for investigative play
- Different textures I.e fabrics, water, sand, playdough
- Weighted blanket or being rolled up in a rug provides a pressure change that can aid regulation
- Tapping locates pressure points around the body to restore balance and reduce stress
- It is important to discuss with the child how they feel after activity

Note: If children are behaving in a way that seems to instigate a physical intervention, they may be seeking pressure based touch.

Activity 3.5
Mindfulness Re-Regulation

Why

Children who are scared or stressed may have excessive amounts of Adrenaline and Cortisol in their system. They may also be overwhelmed by the input around them. Mindfulness activities can be used to ground the child and release negative feelings and chemicals.

The type of mindfulness activity may vary dependent on pupil; some may favour breathing techniques, others may prefer visualisation, whilst others may benefit from physical sensations. They may benefit from a combination, it is vital to meet the individual need of the child and what aids them in relaxing.

What to do

- Choose a type mindfulness activity and create as calm an environment as possible. This may involve changes to lighting, soft music, aromatherapy and soft textures.
- For planned session children to note down, talk about how they feel or even measure heart rate at beginning of session. When rested repeat again at the end.
- Discuss changes in mood after activity.
- Initially activities will be adult led but ultimately these techniques can be used by children as and when they need them for re-regulation

Note: By doing this activity you are not rewarding bad behaviour. It is designed to get the child calm so that the behaviour can be discussed. If a sanction or reparation is needed it should take place after regulated

Activity 3.6
Music Re-Regulation

Why

Children who are scared or stressed may have excessive amounts of Adrenaline and Cortisol in their system. They may also be overwhelmed by the input around them. Music can be a powerful tool in regulation both in terms of releasing negative feelings and emotions and in calming heart rate. The type of music activity may vary dependent on pupil; some may favour listening, others may prefer playing instruments or even singing, whilst others may benefit from writing music or lyrics. It is also possible to teach self-regulation through drum beats. They may benefit from a combination, it is vital to meet the individual need of the child.

What to do

- Choose a simple music beat activity, play and repeat.
- If children are used to music activities allow them to play. Support as required.
- For planned session children to note down, talk about how they feel or even measure heart rate at beginning of session. When rested repeat again at the end.
- Discuss changes in mood after activity.
- Initially activities will be adult led but children will develop the skills and may seek out music activities at times of potential crisis

Note: By doing this activity you are not rewarding bad behaviour. It is designed to get the child calm so that the behaviour can be discussed. If a sanction or reparation is needed it should take place after regulated

BECOMING UNSTUCK

Doing outreach I regularly encounter children who are stuck in a loop. They desperately want to belong but fear rejection. The fear of rejection dysregulates them and they lash out. Other children are rightly wary of them and worry about including them. I talked about Jay at the beginning of the book;

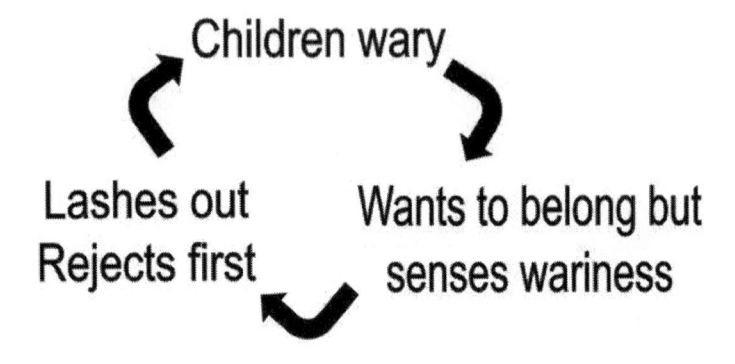

```
        → Children wary ↘
   ↑                        ↓
Lashes out           Wants to belong but
Rejects first  ↙      senses wariness
```

Jay was at completing stage 2 when I saw him. He felt safe in the school environment and trusted his staff. If we complete Stage 3 with Jay he now has the skills to self-regulate and is much less likely to lash out. Children have no reason to be wary of Jay and feel safe to include him. The loop for children like Jay now becomes a line that doesn't result in him being seen as unpredictable and we are set up for stage 4.

RE-REGULATION CONCLUSION

Staff led or pupil led, individual or group, planned or reactive, everytime we co-regulate a child we are showing them how to self-regulate. Every missed opportunity is an opportunity to learn for next time. Just like the baby gets comforted by a caregiver and learns to slow down their heart rate we can recreate this process with music or tapping or even exercising. Fast to begin with then slowing down to calm. We must help children to recognise the process and what has happened to their body, how they felt before the activity and how they feel after. How it changed them.

There are so many variables in a school day. To expect a staff led, pre-emptive intervention every time a child shows any sign of distress is impossible to sustain. Having built in plans for certain children who are known to struggle at certain times of the day can help enormously, as can group activities at certain times like first thing in the morning. These will benefit all children and create calmer learning environments. I think that there are few arguments made by educators that these things are important and beneficial but the reason for not doing it and the excuse for having not done them is always the same. 'We haven't got enough staff/time', 'what about the other children', 'we aren't counselors'.

However the truth is that by teaching the skills together initially they are learning the skill independently. That extra time at the beginning means that the child can now self-regulate which will save us so much intervention time later on. The pay off for that invested time is huge for future learning and wellbeing. Again, the idea of supporting a child who can't read by just handing them books just wouldn't happen. The idea that a staff member would just read to them for the entirety of their school life is unrealistic, resource intensive and time consuming. It also focuses on an immediate solution to a short term problem rather than a long term solution to an underlying problem. Teaching the child to read is what schools would do because they know this makes sense in the long run and empowers the child's learning.

Let's stop short term thinking around behaviour, let's teach it and let's empower those children to control their own emotions, behaviour and learning potential.

> **Pause for thought**- does your setting spend more time managing dysregulated children or teaching them how to regulate themselves?

4. Build Belonging

Chapter 11

FEAR OF REJECTION

We have created a safe environment, built strong adult/child trusting relationships, and equipped children to manage their emotions but we still have a social minefield to negotiate which can have so many barriers to overcome. Even with the best platforms in place, the relationships with peers can be a huge challenge; trying to work out what people think, how we are perceived, whether we are liked, how do we impress people. These are things that adults, with fully developed brains are trying to figure out everyday. It causes us stress, it makes us second guess and it prevents us from doing things. What others think and whether we will be accepted or rejected plays a huge role in our lives and that is assuming we have had the opportunities to succeed.

So what if we haven't had those opportunities to succeed in relationships with peers?

What if critical skills for negotiating this minefield weren't learned?

Anyone who has ever experienced a toddler group will be aware of what a full on war zone those places can be. There's snatching, there's hitting, there's screaming and crying, but behind the organised chaos there is an abundance of learning. Children learn how to share toys, they learn how to take turns, they learn how to share adult attention, how to manage their emotions and most importantly they learn about friendships and belonging. They overcome the animalistic urges to dominate and mark territory and replace them with a desire for community. In a safe environment led by an adult these very young children figure out belonging and equip themselves for a future nursery/reception environment.

Unfortunately for many children this phase of development is all too often being missed. I've watched in frustration as younger and younger children are at risk of exclusion before completing Key Stage 1. I hear them described as violent and written off at an age where their education journey has barely begun. The blame for this often falls on 'soft' parenting but I believe environmental factors influence the children's experiences enormously and parents often need support not judgement.

Whether it's;

- the fact that parents are more likely to be separated from their own families than in the past meaning less support
- less playing with cousins
- cuts to family support services - For example Homestart who would have offered those toddler groups
- the increase in technology which can be used to occupy and entertain young children with minimal effort and interaction.

The likelihood is a combination of all these factors to create a perfect storm that leaves children totally unprepared for that first day at school. These children aren't violent and shouldn't be excluded, They are overwhelmed and should be taught how to include themselves and others.

Just like other elements of behaviour we cannot punish children for not learning something they have never been taught!

Whether it is boundaries that are missing or if it's the social skills or if it's both. Nothing is gained by being frustrated at parents, we have to understand why those behaviours are happening and replace the missing skills. Just like we would any gaps in academic learning.

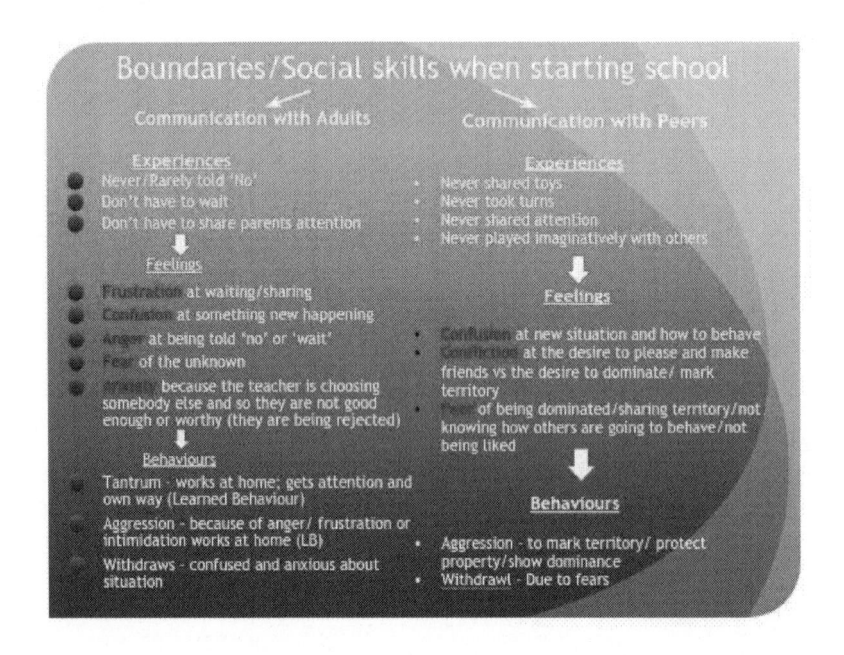

Boundaries/Social skills when starting school

Communication with Adults

Experiences
- Never/Rarely told 'No'
- Don't have to wait
- Don't have to share parents attention

Feelings
- Frustration at waiting/sharing
- Confusion at something new happening
- Anger at being told "no" or 'wait'
- Fear of the unknown
- Anxiety because the teacher is choosing somebody else and so they are not good enough or worthy (they are being rejected)

Behaviours
- Tantrum - works at home; gets attention and own way (Learned Behaviour)
- Aggression - because of anger/ frustration or intimidation works at home (LB)
- Withdraws - confused and anxious about situation

Communication with Peers

Experiences
- Never shared toys
- Never took turns
- Never shared attention
- Never played imaginatively with others

Feelings
- Confusion at new situation and how to behave
- Confliction at the desire to please and make friends vs the desire to dominate/ mark territory
- Fear of being dominated/sharing territory/not knowing how others are going to behave/not being liked

Behaviours
- Aggression - to mark territory/ protect property/show dominance
- Withdrawl - Due to fears

BOUNDARIES

So if on the first day of reception a child walks in who hasn't ever encountered an environment involving other children and is used to having an adult always available and few boundaries. They may have very limited **experiences**;

- never really been told 'no'
- they have rarely been asked to wait for anything
- never had to share adult attention

Suddenly being faced with boundaries and expectations and all the other children competing for an adults attention can create a lot of different **feelings**;

- Being asked to wait will be very frustrating
- This alien environment will be very confusing
- Being told no might make them feel angry
- Going from having a reasonable amount of control at home to having none might cause a lot of fear
- Seeing the adult spending time with another child rather than them may cause the perception that the other child is better, that they are themselves less important or less worthy. This can bring anxiety and affect self-esteem

Faced with all these negative feelings the child reaches into their own toolbox of strategies to best manage these feelings and this situation. The **behaviour** they choose will likely be;

- A tantrum/aggression usually works at home to get attention and their own way
- Withdraw from the situation and hide what they are feeling

Young children may find it harder to suppress their feelings than older ones and may become overwhelmed. This is also likely to come out as aggression like in the train line.

SOCIAL SKILLS

Equally, the absence of interaction with other children of the same age will mean that their **experiences** are unlikely to have prepared them for this school environment;

- They have never had to share toys
- Never had to take turns
- Never had to compete for attention or be heard
- They may never have played imaginatively with others, especially if the play they have experienced involved electronic devices

All tools in the child's individual "tool box" would have been learned in toddler groups or nursery and brought to school. Without them the child will fill that box with negative feelings;

- They will be confused at how to follow these unofficial rules that the other children seem to know and how to play with others
- On one hand they will still have a desire to dominate and mark territory (they haven't yet learned that this isn't needed) on the other they desperately want to belong and be part of the group. This leaves them very conflicted
- They are scared to give up their territory to others, scared that they will be rejected by the group and scared that they don't understand the play

This mixture of feelings is very overwhelming. The **behaviours** are likely to be;

- Aggression; either to assert dominance or mark territory. The behaviours the toddlers display at 18

months are still displayed at age 4/5. It could also be because they are overwhelmed and can't control it
- They may feel they can't negotiate this environment and withdraw. Not being involved is a better option than being rejected

THE POWER OF PLAY

I'll never forget very early into my days in what was then an EBD setting, I was asked to support the after school club. I had an exciting time planned with the trampoline out and various other activities. When I went to collect the children from a classroom what I saw really took me by surprise, despite there being games consoles, pool tables and a dart board. 3 15 year old boys were playing with toy cars on a road mat. Not just messing either, fully engaged in imaginative play with each other. Communication, turn taking and sharing liked I'd never had in one of my lessons. They were so engrossed they didn't even notice me arrive and had little interest in my trampoline offer.

Being quite new and quite surprised by what I was seeing I'd asked the more experienced member of staff about it. Caroline was that staff member who had been at the school since it was built and is still there 15 years on. She is built into the fabric of the building and leaves a mark on every adult and child that walks through the door. She went on to explain that all three boys were rejected and had had nothing in their early development, they'd never just played and were just meeting a need that had never been met. The issue is that they would never show it in front of their class for fear of what they would think, in this environment after school with others they trust they are safe to play however they need to.

This unmet need has been visible in so many children over the last decade and just like with any unmet need it doesn't go away until we meet it. Every now and again one of our children would ask if they could go and "mentor" in our primary department. We would usually be happy to accommodate this, but when I would get feedback from the staff in primary about what a helpful mentor they had been, I would often get the same response.

"They didn't want to mentor, they just wanted to play with their stuff!"

They barely acknowledged the primary children but they played alongside. With the lego, the cars or the figures. Sure, I'd have rather some genuine mentoring took place but if that need has now been met and that helps them to learn for the rest of the day, then it is far from wasted time.

REJECT FIRST

Many children I have worked with have been in this position. Over time new behaviours and survival strategies are learned and children become very skilled at controlling what happens and masking the real difficulties. By withdrawing and behaving aggressively it often brings unwanted attention or consequences. How we react to these early warning signs and unlearnt skills play a huge part in the child's development. The sooner we meet the needs and give them the tools, the sooner we remove the fear, confusion, confliction, frustration and anxiety from that child's relationship with their peer group.

If we focus on the aggression without teaching the skills, the child will need to find other ways to avoid getting into trouble and avoid failure and rejection. 'You can't fail at something if you don't try it'. The safest way to avoid rejection and to stay in control is to be the one who rejects. The child will develop emotional "masks" in an effort to avoid or control the rejection.

MASK 1 - THE REJECTOR

One mask the child will adopt is to push other children away because then they will never have to be the one pushed away. They stay in that comfort zone because even though it is lonely they have control over it and letting other children in is too scary. By rejecting, they never have to manage those emotions of relationships breaking down.

The longer this continues the more skilled the masking becomes. However the further into childhood the more social children become. By accepting this sabotaging of relationships rather than challenging it, meeting those early needs and teaching the skills needed for belonging we accept the likelihood that the child will not be happy, not achieve their potential and not have the skills for successful relationships in adulthood.

As educators we have to be prepared to challenge this idea with the child at whatever stage of their education we have them. The earlier the better but it is never too late and we should never accept it. Of course some children are more sociable than others but every child needs to belong. We must teach missed skills and meet missed needs in order to help them achieve this if we want that child to be successful in their learning and in their life.

ANDY'S SABOTAGE

Andy was tall, stocky and very awkward. His unkempt mousy blonde hair, trousers too short and bobbly jumper. He would only give you tiny bits of info about his past and wasn't forthcoming with information about his present. The only time Andy would appear happy was if he was pleased by someone else's misfortune. He rarely joined in, didn't share laughter with others, only laughed at them and appeared to make himself feel better by making others feel worse. Whenever another child would attempt to work with him or befriend him in any way he would be unpleasant to them until they gave up or even better got angry with him. He seemed to find it a success if he got others to lash out at him.

He had learned to mask his loneliness with unpleasantness. The adults had let him down in his life but so had the other children. He'd gone into care because of neglectful parents, they'd never been available for him, never taken him anywhere and never played with him. His only early life experience of other children was a one year older brother who had cared for him more than his parents. When Andy was taken into care the siblings were separated. Andy had spent time in care homes where he had been described as a 'loner', 'doesn't play well with others', 'enjoys others hurting him'. School reports were a similar story for Andy. He didn't have friends but didn't seem to want any. He behaved well generally with staff, especially 1 to 1, but his behaviour with peers was poor.

As Andy's form teacher the challenge for me wasn't just to get Andy to let his own guard down and let other children in, it was convincing the other children that his behaviour towards them wasn't because he disliked them but was because he feared them. It took a long time to get him to understand what he was doing. He was doing separate social story work to help him understand why he feared rejection, when calm and regulated he admitted he wanted it to change but he didn't know how. He'd been sabotaging relationships for so long it was second nature. Other children were waiting for the insult or unpleasant remark to come and he would often oblige. The child 1 to 1 and the child in a group were completely different.

We started with paired work. I had another child who struggled to fit in and tolerated Andy's behaviour more than others. We tried teacher led intervention that was fun and seeking out a common interest. It happened to be cycling and although it wasn't easy and it was often 1 step forward 2 steps back we had the 2 children interacting. When in class there was a reduction of unpleasantness from Andy. The paired work became small group work, often with bike riding as a reward. We were able to do group discussion and have breakfast together as a group without Andy sabotaging it. He was never going to be popular amongst his peer group because there was too much history there but he could co-exist and now he could go to college for a fresh start with a clean slate equipped with skills to build relationships and with some control over his fear of rejection.

The intervention for Andy came too late. He was in an alien environment, felt let down and abandoned by his brother and didn't want to feel those feelings again so pushed everyone away. If someone had identified the motivation for his behaviour and reacted with empathy and understanding, if they had met the needs and replaced the missing social skills early in his school life I am confident Andy wouldn't have been perceived the way he was. He wanted to belong but convinced everybody he didn't. It was better for him to be miserable and lonely than to risk feeling again the way he did when he was split from his brother. For Andy we managed to help him realise that the feeling of belonging was worth the risk, this couldn't be done by telling him, it had to be done by showing him and getting him to experience it and feel it.

MASK 2 - THE MANIPULATOR

For some children the best way to hide the fear of rejection is to see others as something to control rather than to open up to. By seeing yourself as superior to others and controlling their behaviour it takes away unpredictability and vulnerability. By putting themselves above others they don't have to be genuine and can play a character which hides the real personality that they believe deep down will be rejected. Some children will use intimidation to maintain this position and are excellent at selling themselves as super confident and a leader. They are often seen as bullies.

The truth is that it is a mask. The belief that if the other children were ever to see what is behind the mask then they wouldn't want to be associated with them and they would be rejected.

RICHIE'S LEADERSHIP

Richie was a very skilled athlete, handsome, appeared popular and intelligent. He was a voice that could always be heard and always front and centre of an entourage. He presented as egocentric, confident and cocky whenever he was around others. If he found work challenging he would often refuse and encourage others to follow his lead. This behaviour had led to his exclusion for persistent disruptive behaviour.

He lived with his grandad due to his mum's alcohol and drug use. He had an older brother who had been in and out of prison for violence related offences whom he was very scared of, although he would never admit that in front of anyone. Individually and with trusted adults, Ritchie would share his passions and be open about his home circumstances. He could articulate how he felt when he was calm and regulated. However he had no peers with whom he shared this information.

Over time it became clear that the dynamic of the relationship with the other pupils was not one of friendship. When talking to the other children individually they often referred to Ritchie as 'cool' or 'sound' but they were intimidated by him. Ritchie himself had learned a lot of intimidation skills from his older brother that he used on his peer group, because he was intelligent he could manipulate others and use them for his own entertainment. He admitted that he did this for a buzz but it wasn't really satisfying. It was the character he played and it made him feel safe to have control over others. He believed if he showed any weakness then others would treat him the way his brother does. He would occasionally admit to being really physically tired of pretending but was too scared to change.

The one place Ritchie dropped the act was playing football at break times. We would have a big range of age groups playing which would change the social dynamic. He was so good he didn't need an act. The older children had respect for his ability, the younger ones were in awe of him. He would get fouled regularly but understand it was because he was too skillful and too fast, so he didn't react angry and aggressively. Coaching these younger children became part of Ritchie's plan. He didn't feel threatened by them and didn't need to intimidate to get their respect. He thrived doing it and he and some of his peer group took on a sports leader qualification. What he wanted to achieve outweighed the fear and the group thrived. He was still the leader but not through the mask and not through intimidation. He became a very strong captain of the football team using encouragement rather than fear to get the best out of the team. The role of mentor for younger children crossed over from just football and he became house captain. Children looking up to him, not because he was tough, but because they cared what he thought.

The mask would still return in times of crisis around children his own age and I would be lying if I said he stopped the intimidation tactics altogether but Ritchie went to college to complete a sports leader course and go on to be a football coach. He found a place where he could be himself and channelled it in a positive way. I hope he lets more people in and can be himself in the future.

MASK 3 - THE CLASS CLOWN

'If everyone is laughing at me then they must like me'. This was said to me by a relatively new pupil when I asked them why they had spent an English lesson interrupting the teacher with Whale noises. The idea that any attention is better than no attention, bouncing from one social group to the next and never really being in a friendship group but always on the periphery. Doing silly, risk taking things for approval but being laughed at, rather than laughed with.

Many children who do these things are still trying to figure out the same things they were trying to figure out that first day of reception. Desperately wanting to belong but trying to find a shortcut to get them there. Often getting themselves into copious amounts of trouble along the way. When you ask children to describe another child and they describe their actions not their personality it is usually a sign of a social skills problem.

DEN'S RISK TAKING

Den was medium height, medium build, was intelligent when he applied himself and funny when he wanted to be. He'd been in and out of care and everytime he got settled somewhere his mum would want him back then it would break down and he'd have to start all over again. Everything was blamed on Den's behaviour by Mum. 'See what he's doing', 'well if you do that you are choosing to go back into care' or 'why can't you just be like your brother'. Den was on the autistic spectrum and we strongly suspected ADHD also, though both were possibly a result of the rejection trauma. He struggled to see the impact of his behaviours, the perspectives of others and he lacked impulse control and consequential thinking.

When he had come to us he had distanced himself from adult relationships also. He would damage things in his care home to push them away and focussed on material goods rather than relationships. He always talked about designer clothes, not always one he'd bought, Den had been caught shoplifting numerous times. He would use these to try to impress kids but he had no close relationships. He would do things to show off and was more interested in a quick laugh than anything meaningful. He treated others more as an audience than a group of peers.

He had built some positive relationships with staff. He shared a love of mountain biking with the Headteacher and it created trust and a safe place for Den to go. He would get overwhelmed at times but on the whole managed his emotions well although his general mood was very low. He responded to the structure and consistency of school and was interested in learning, although well below where he should have been. He was referred to by others as 'funny' and 'mad' but bounced from group to group, sitting somewhere different with a different group each day at lunch. The overconfident show off working the room as if the laughter was fuel.

Outside school he would overcome the negative feelings with short term buzzes by doing stupid and outragous things to get the attention of peers and to escape what he was feeling. Different risk taking behaviour each week; jumping trains, shoplifting, drinking, drug taking and underage sex. Yet unless he was missing from the care home he would come to school and cope ok. He would brag about the things he was doing and get a bit of attention but not as much as he really wanted.

We took Den on a residential and it gave him a chance to bond with the group. His risk taking could be managed through activities and he could gain shots of approval by showing off skills during them. He had already escaped what awaited him at home so he could relax a bit and children saw a different side to him. They would be more interested in his mountain biking than his mad weekend in Blackpool.

Sadly, Den was moved to a care placement out of area before we could complete the work we were trying to do with him but I believe if we could have had more time we could have built on that camp experience. We had some green shoots of belonging that I wish we could have nurtured.

EVERY CHILD NEEDS TO BELONG

Sometimes it is too scary and the risk of rejection outweighs the need to belong but it doesn't mean it isn't there. It doesn't mean the child is happy being a loner despite what they may tell us, and it should never be accepted. I've met many children who will never be comfortable in big groups but they are the happiest I have ever seen them with a small group of like minded individuals. One of the greatest things we can do as educators is to facilitate this happening. Looking back at my career thus far when I think about my proudest achievements, none were in the classroom. The classroom successes came from the work elsewhere and if there is one thing I have learned, it is that whatever the children may say, however great the fear of rejection may be, they all want to belong!

LEVI AND RENE'S UNLIKELY BROMANCE

Levi was by far and away the grumpiest child I had ever met. I genuinely mean that in an affectionate way, if Eyore was a child he would have been Levi. He moved in the same loping style, shoulders hunched like he was carrying the world. The first question I ever asked him was about the things he liked and his answer was very clear 'I like animals, I just hate people'! He was very clear about this and was consistent throughout his first term. He would tolerate the adults and avoid the children. He would look for any excuse to get home, absconding on occasion.

I can joke about Levi's demeanour now and by the time he left us so could he, however his reasons for feeling like that weren't funny. He had huge social difficulties, had suffered terrible bullying and his experiences of adults weren't much better. Levi's mum had Bi-Polar disorder, made worse by the actions of his alcoholic older brother. Her inconsistency had led him to withdraw from her and everyone else had followed.

Levi was a skilled school refuser and had nothing in school that he was interested in and no future goals. He wanted to be in his house with his cat and his self esteem was lower on the floor. He had decided he had Autism, was going to have Bi-Polar and would hurt people because he couldn't control himself.

Changing this mindset was no small task and it needed to start small. We built a relationship with Mum so we could encourage from both sides. Mum's experience of schools had been constant threats of fines with little by way of support. When we had this we started to bring him in. The only thing that had interested him during our tour of the school was the rabbits roaming the back field. The only subject where he hadn't replied 'I hate ....' was food tech. The food tech classroom overlooked the back field so Levi started to reluctantly attend a lesson a day in there. He would cook for a bit and watch the rabbits. Then he would cook for a bit and have a walk outside to see the rabbits. Then as things progressed he would do other subject work with the cookery teacher.

One of my pastoral team would be in and out of these sessions building some rapport with Levi. To build on the sessions he suggested some Art sessions. 'I reeaalllly hate Art' was Levi's response to this suggestion. Tom simply will not have that, so kept plugging away at Levi. He wouldn't paint or draw so they made things and crafted. They started to work on themes led by Levi, realising that he had a huge interest in conservation and recycling. They started an art project that crossed over into other subjects.

The thing about Tom is that he has always found a way in with children regardless of their interests. He has always been a conundrum to me. On one hand a lead singer in a band with his long hair, tattoos and lost razor making him cool and current to the kids. On the other hand a total geek with encyclopedic knowledge of Star Wars, Pokemon and Dragonball Z. It was Dragonball Z which was the common ground and the hook for Tom with Levi. Not only in conversation but an anime art style that would get Levi to pick up a paintbrush.

The cooking reduced and the art became the hook, as much because it gave him the chance to talk interests with Tom as it did the subject. Tom was able to reduce time to be replaced by other staff and other subjects but still regularly checking in, regular pauses for a political discussion on climate change. Levi still wouldn't join a peer group but would work at the back of the room while other classes had lessons, occasionally joining in but no longer feeling threatened. He was now attending daily for half days and not trying to get home at every opportunity. It was a term in and he still hadn't smiled but we'd had humour and "I still hate it, it's still pointless, but it's better than my last school."

Take the win!

Rene had been really successful in the early part of his time in school. Shorter than average, jet black hair and friendly in nature he had been a keen learner, talented athlete and stunning artist. Rene had a mental health crisis midway through year 9 that blew his school life out of the water. He had much to try and manage, became almost agoraphobic and the effect on his opinion of self was catastrophic. He pushed away children who had been friends and teachers he'd had good relationships with. Getting him back into school was my job and I was failing miserably. The only thing that was helping him cope outside school was art. His sketchbook was always in his hand. Filled with dark, Gothic but truly brilliant drawings. In a moment of utter desperation I suggested we try to put Rene with Levi and Tom and see if they could co-exist.

It was sheer dumb luck but it worked brilliantly. At first Rene would sit in silence doing art while Tom and Levi talked Dragonball Z. It was perfect for Levi because there was no pressure to try and engage with the other pupils, it was perfect for Rene because no-one was pressuring him for interaction. Rene secretly started to share an interest in the conversations about anime, he was able to produce quite amazing pieces of anime art which interested Levi. The boys started to interact. Tom was able to take a step back. The boys would motivate each other, help each other and very occasionally get the other to complete work. It was a slog but time in school for both increased, work was minimal but was happening and we had smiles and laughter from both boys. They even started to join their own peers for some lessons.

Outside school the boys would even meet up outside of school. Both got good art GCSEs, Levi a B and Rene an A*, together with enough other qualifications and both went on to college together. Levi admitted upon leaving that he 'still hates most people, still prefers animals, but it's good to have a friend'. I expect these two to find other children at college to grow this microgroup, but what we achieved with those two boys will always be high on my achievement list.

I know the counter-argument will always be that this was too many resources and time needed for too few pupils which I completely understand, but Levi came to us in year 10. How many opportunities for less in depth intervention had been passed up, how many times did he have to fail in order to get the support he needed, each one ingraining the negative perspective on school. Despite everything he thought he believed about himself, the reality is that he did want to belong, he did care about others and he didn't have to continue in the misery comfort zone he was in. If he'd been equipped with those belonging skills earlier that failure, and his misery, could have been avoided.

TEACHING SOCIAL SKILLS

There are many good Social Skills packages on the market. My school used the 'Talkabout' package by Alex Kelly. It was an excellent scaffold for working with children to increase their skills recognising body language, having conversations and levels of assertiveness. We were able to create a safe environment from which children could try out these new skills. What it also gave the children was the opportunity to recognise that they weren't alone in finding these scenarios hard. This had a positive impact on their self esteem and helped them to engage, learning together in a safe environment. The talkabout wheels allowed for an assessment to help focus areas to work on and show improvement. In a world where everything has to be data, this is a very useful tool to have.

We knew that the children were extremely worried about what other children thought, this is very natural for children, especially adolescents. What we weren't prepared for was how much they misperceived the actions of others and how much they couldn't understand why other children didn't understand their intentions. Poor attempts at humour or using 'I'm only joking' to excuse a multitude of unpleasant behaviours was commonplace. It was a get out of free card and obviously there were children who did this deliberately to get away with insulting someone. However more commonly it was 'Oh no I've got it wrong, if I say i'm joking no-one will notice'.

We'd thought for a while that 'only joking' was a planned excuse to be unpleasant but it appeared it was a response to an ill thought out comment that had back-fired. This meant the motive was different which meant our responses needed to be.

The children knew enough from their peers' body language to know they had caused offence and upset them but they didn't know why. By staff responding to the comment itself and saying things like 'but it isn't funny', we just confirm the part the child has already figured out, what we haven't done is given them any help to understand why.

Instead we should respond by teaching the child why they have caused offence. Teaching children to understand the perspective of others is a difficult task for adults, it's challenging for young children but it's hardest when you have an adolescent brain. When you naturally become more egocentric following puberty the adolescent brain makes seeing others point of view less important. However for the child fighting to belong it is vital. So supplementing the basic social skills learned through talkabout with constant opportunities to analyse communication mistakes became staple. It was still important for the comments to be challenged but the teaching took priority. To do this effectively it is important to have a level of understanding of how the adolescent brain works.

SELFISH, THOUGHTLESS AND DANGEROUS

These are words often used to describe teenagers. It's almost understood enough to be expected of them but not accepted enough for them not to be criticised, judged and punished for it. Many teachers and parents have very short memories and forget the decisions they made when they were younger were most likely as bad, if not worse. They will also have been worse when in the company of their peers. What others think is the driving force for most adolescent decision making. It is why some are more likely to show off to gain approval and why others avoid this in fear of disapproval, but make no mistake about it, in the moment, what we think as adults and the potential consequences hasn't had a look in.

Sarah-Jayne Blakemore is a leading scientist studying the adolescent brain and her book 'Inventing Ourselves' goes into great detail about adolescent child behaviour. I believe an understanding of it is critical to explaining children's actions and why zero tolerance fails in secondary settings.

If what others think is more important than the threat and consequence, then increasing the threat won't matter.

We have to find another way to change behaviour. If the driving force is belonging and approval of others, let's teach ways to get this that doesn't require negative behaviour. Let's not make them choose between following the rules and gaining peer approval, let's offer both. Just like we did with Jamie, Richie and Den. They weren't bothered by the consequences of their actions, each had kept behaving worse until they were excluded. The punitive approach had failed them. It was showing them that they had other ways to gain approval that didn't involve a mask and didn't involve risk taking or poor behaviour.

The thing with adolescents is that we focus so much on the negative aspects we miss the positives. The emotional part of the brain hasn't fully developed so they feel things more intensely and seek out shots of feel good dopamine, but the thinking part isn't there yet meaning the thoughts about consequences aren't there. This has obvious problems but it also means that adolescents have passion and creativity in abundance. I know the current curriculum isn't designed to nurture this but that doesn't mean we shouldn't. The reduced arts curriculum is a huge frustration for many in education.

We all want children to behave perfectly but most adolescents are focussed on themselves and what's in it for them. We can fight it or accept it but given a choice between a child risk taking and misbehaving to gain peer approval versus a child using their passion and creativity channelled into something positive in order to gain it, I know what I would choose.

Caring deeply what others think doesn't go away as we get older either. I'm writing this book and I can claim otherwise as much as I like but I will care what people think. I am still nervous every time I do a course and I'm still outraged by what I feel are unfair evaluations. The difference between 39 year old me and 16 year old me is the fact I am more able to rationalise. 16 year old me would have feared rejection and kept quiet. Reviews may very well prove 16 year old me right!

SOCIAL ISOLATION AS PUNISHMENT

I've reiterated many times that knowing the motive behind behaviour is key to preventing it. The problem with this is when the motivation is used to create a punishment. Young children want something, we take it away as punishment when they misbehave; sweets, toys, time playing. It wouldn't be my choice of sanction because it is more about control than teaching but with younger children sanctions are generally less severe and there is very little the child can do to fight back against it and so the impact is lessened. This very simplistic rewards and sanction based response is very common in schools I've worked with and a go to for the DfE.

If this is our tool then we are going to adopt the same approach with older children, we know that the adolescent child is driven by social inclusion, so what better consequence to get them to behave than social exclusion. It worked before it should work now. The problem is that they aren't little children anymore and can't be controlled as easily. One of the other features of adolescence is not backing down to authority. Young children care more about what the adults think than what the other children think. Your misbehaving adolescent values your opinion far less than that of their peers.

If the initial sanction/threat of sanction has been ineffective, this is when the choice becomes to either back down and take a different approach, or to escalate the sanction. Spend any time on Social Media and you will come across a parent who doesn't know what to do because in a moment of madness has grounded their children for a decade. Desperately torn between wanting to reduce it but not wanting to be seen backing down. Similarly in schools the use of isolation as punishment and the disproportionate increases in length of time because an hour, a day or a week didn't work.

Paul Dix talks about the failures of giving recognition to the poor behaviours, celebrity status to the child that doesn't conform. Whilst we give fame to the child that did a month in isolation we are also causing them damage and creating a persona they must live up to. We have created a scenario by which they must choose risk of harm vs risk of rejection. Inconsequential thinking, lack of impulse control and an absence of critical thinking will nearly always choose risk of harm.

So let's not make it a choice!

SOCIAL ISOLATION TO SUPPORT

The research done by Sarah-Jayne Blakemore and her associates demonstrated how adolescents behaved differently around their peers. If this is the case and they have a persona or mask in place, then isolating them from the peer group is vital to discuss the behaviour. We would occasionally have a group of kids who had separately struggled in class and left the room. Unfortunately they would meet up at a time when none were regulated and none were thinking through their actions and they would escalate each other's behaviours. We would know as a pastoral team that the only way to get these children back was to split them up. Until we did this no attempt to calm, communicate or threaten would matter. Often described as a pack mentality, all actions are done to get approval of the others without thought of consequences. No rational thought is being used. What the other child perceived was absolutely more important than us.

If we could isolate from each other we could get their thinking brain back. Then we would have a choice to make. We could punish or we could understand. Again we shouldn't ignore the behaviour and if reparations are needed then they should happen but what was the child's need and motivation. If it was getting approval from peers for being disrespectful or not conforming to authority then we need to find a more positive method for them to gain peer approval, having them away from the group allows for that discussion to take place without risk of peer judgement. The children will have often naturally, have already created an us and them mentality, we must accept it and overcome it not encourage it.

If the motivation is to avoid looking stupid or being found out and rejected then we need to offer the necessary support to prevent this feeling. It is only when this fear is truly gone that our children have a chance to fulfil their learning potential.

> **Pause for thought - How is social isolation being used in your setting?**

5. Foster Courage/Vulnerability

Chapter 12

BRAVE LEARNERS

"Choose courage over comfort. Choose whole hearts over armour and choose the great adventure of being brave and afraid at the exact same time." Brene Brown

It is hard to pick out just one quote from Brene Brown on this area. One thing she is clear on is that we achieve nothing in life without making ourselves vulnerable first. Every decision we make requires courage. We have to risk failure, we have to risk looking stupid and we have to risk rejection. For many children this is too much and it's safer not to try. Same is true in adult life; if you never turn up, you never ask anyone on a date, you never go to the job interview, do the speech or ask someone to marry you, then it significantly limits the potential for happiness and fulfilment, which I believe should be the priority goal for all children.

Even if happiness and fulfilment isn't our priority, even if our priority is purely the GCSE grade, they stand a far better chance if we have given them all the tools.

THE TEST

It doesn't matter our school culture, our ethos, whether we are zero tolerance or extremely nurturing, school still ends in the same way. They still sit the exam, they still have to remember the information and they still have to take all the risks. We can supplement courses and qualifications to try to relieve the pressure but the children still have to put themselves out there for judgement. There is so much more to passing an exam than being intelligent or having a good memory. Safety, calm and self belief are equally if not more important.

The very fact we put the tests at the beginning of and the very height of adolescence, at the point where children are hypersensitive to the judgement of others, is one of the reasons so many children struggle with their mental health at exam time. We often are comfortable waving this away as 'exam stress' that will go away, but maybe we should be asking ourselves whether we have done enough to equip our children with the tools to manage this. Being ready for an exam often means they have been inputted with all of the information, but what if being exam ready is just as much about having the tools to manage the stressful environment. Putting stress into the mix when we don't have safety means we don't have calm, if we don't have calm then we can't think fully, if we can't think fully we cannot achieve our potential on an exam.

We don't see exams as a holistic process, just an academic one. I've seen teachers comment on children who have disappointed in exams 'they knew it all, they should have done better', 'I did my job, they've let themselves down', 'You can lead a horse to water'. We shouldn't be ok with accepting that children have 'bottled it' in the exam. We should want to know why and analyse why.

- Did we do enough to reduce the fear of failure?
- Did we teach the child the skills to manage stressful situations?
- Did we concentrate enough on building belief?
- Did we teach the child to be courageous?

These questions should be answered upon the end of every child's school journey. Making sure we can answer yes will mean children will be able to achieve their potential in those exams and take forward the courage to overcome vulnerability in future aspects of their lives. The things I have talked about in this book don't prioritise the academic and there will be those that will argue that doing the things I have suggested detracts from valuable learning time.

However, what if the side effect of the holistic sequential approach is a child who is able to sit an exam without fear meaning they aren't worried what people will think, a child who feels calm and can access their thought processes and memory more effectively, and what about the fact that they have so many successes to draw up on, given the confidence to really believe they can do well.

How invaluable are these skills come SATs/GCSE day?

> **<u>Pause for thought</u> - would results be better in your setting if all the building blocks were in place?**

RED FLAGS?

It is common to expect children to make themselves vulnerable in school everyday. We know that the best way to increase academic knowledge is to push them. We create a small amount of stress, we expect mistakes and we learn from the corrections. We expect children to answer questions in front of entire groups of peers even when they are unsure of the answers and even single them out even though we are fairly sure they don't know.

Would we do this to adults?

Would we be happy if it was done to us in a staff meeting?

Not looking stupid in front of our adult colleagues is anxiety inducing enough but we put children in the position of looking stupid in front of their peers on a regular basis and we have to acknowledge the impact of this. Asking the class to answer questions is an important part of confirming understanding but it should be voluntary. If we aren't sure that a child has understood, there are other ways of finding out that doesn't involve singling them out in front of the group. It will be counter productive in the long run.

I have talked a lot throughout the book about children using behaviour to mask and avoid work. The child who would rather misbehave or walk out than face failure. However there are other ways children can mask. We may have created a safe environment by removing threat, we may have removed a fear of rejection by peers but we still have to overcome a lack of self-belief.

We still have to overcome the fear of failure.

THE CAMOUFLAGED

Classes are full of children who just do enough. They will complete the task they have been set but you never feel to the best of their ability. They never take the lead in their learning and when it comes to assessment they are always graded lower than you think they should be. It may be that this child still fears the rejection of looking stupid or it may be an autistic trait of taking the instructions very literally. However, often children use mediocrity as camouflage to avoid risk, if we have put all the building blocks of the sequential approach in place, then it is likely self belief that is the barrier.

We all encounter situations everyday that present them with a choice;

Do they take a risk or do they play safe?

Can they control the outcome or do they have to leave some of it to chance?

There are those that will play safe, control as much as they can, whereas others will relinquish control. Some will stick to what they know and where they are comfortable, others will risk being uncomfortable and risk the unknown. Having the choice, the time to think about the decisions and the opportunity to discuss decisions with others we trust means that the adult can come to an informed decision, made calmly, with the support of others.

Does the adult believe that they themselves can do it?

Do others believe they can do it?

With time to think and the support of others this often leads to a calculated risk being taken. For adults if they were asked to respond immediately to risk taking situations, many would decide against it.

Children often don't have this. Thinking time and the opportunity to discuss with others are luxuries they don't have in school, therefore they must make a decision on impulse based on previous learning experiences. Which often leads to them playing it safe. Just like Molly with her behaviour decision making being worse when put on the spot due to all the failed experiences in her bag. Making children choose immediately from a bag of failed learning experiences, will create a 'playing it safe' learning environment where fear of failure outweighs the potential for success. If we want them to take risks in their learning environment then they have to believe they can succeed based on their experiences. The likelihood of success informs every decision we make. If we want children to take risks in their learning, we have to make them believe that risk will succeed.

JAVID THE CHAMELEON

Javid was the master of camouflage in class. Very rarely misbehaving, never seeking out praise, avoiding answering questions wherever possible. From talking to him he was clearly intelligent and articulate. His work was always completed but it would be hard to get him to do extra or improve it. He saw himself as nothing special, was totally comfortable with that and didn't aspire to be anything else.

He lived in a tiny space, things would be said at home in the heat of the moment and he would overhear conversations where he was called stupid by family members and told he would amount to nothing. His parents' experience of school had been negative so he was told that it was a waste of time. He would get it done and then work in a shop or collect benefits as soon as possible. No further education, no career, no point, no belief he could achieve anything else. At a previous school he had started to complete his work to a higher standard but his teacher had started to try and push him, talking about a positive future and challenging the narrative he had of himself. When he withdrew from this because it challenged what he believed, his apathy was taken as laziness and this was said to him in front of his parents. Rather than using his intelligence to continue to build him up and believe he could be better, the teacher's frustration had made it a tool to shame him further and use against him, having things he enjoyed taken away because he wasn't trying . It caused a huge deterioration in his behaviour as he became more and more excluded from school life.

When he arrived at our school he had totally withdrawn. However he very quickly embraced the new setting. He felt secure and his polite, calm demeanour was a hit with staff. Surrounded by strong characters it was relatively easy to go unnoticed, He had a small group of friends and was fairly invisible to the rest but staff were realising that there was much more Javid could achieve. Changing a mindset takes time and his barriers needed to be overcome. He now believed trying hard would mean repeating what happened at Primary again so he worked hard to hide and blend in.

He was able to complete the work whilst simultaneously working out the average speed at which others completed their's and make sure he was somewhere in the middle. This is a safety tactic children up and down the country use. We had to make him believe in himself, that he wasn't like his parents and that he did have a say in his future. He may well be used to and accepting of the situation he is in and the life map set out for him but that doesn't mean he has to be. We were simultaneously supporting Mum and the family had moved from caravan park to house. She was starting to believe things could be different.

College wasn't on the cards for Javid, university a ridiculous notion but we knew he was capable. The question was could we transfer our belief in him to make him believe in himself. Could we get mum to back us and help her child take a chance with his learning. Dad had left but was still a barrier, everytime we would lift Javid up, Dad would knock him back down. Good work done by Mum would be undone during rows between parents that Javid overheard. Although we were taking 1 step forward and 2 back at times the approach and language was consistent. Building the stress and risk taking in learning slowly, subtly praising but never in front of peers. He now talks about college and a career although he has no idea what it will be. For us that doesn't matter it's the belief that counts and the courage to try.

Javid will definitely achieve the grades to do the college course of his choice, I hope and believe he will go.

THE PERFECTIONIST

> *"When perfectionism is driving, shame is riding shotgun, and fear is that annoying backseat driver."*
> Brene Brown

Perfectionism is not a healthy thing for a child to have. It's the kind of thing that often gets flippantly dismissed but is extremely damaging to wellbeing and learning. Children who do not feel that they can make mistakes will not take risks and will self shame on a regular basis. It can drive pessimism and an ingrained belief that it is better not to try. The necessary stress of pushing learning will be rejected and avoided by this child. They are having an internal battle that we cannot affect with external consequences. We have to change the child's mindset, we have to do this by showing them everybody makes mistakes, everybody is human.

Perfectionism is common with children on the Autistic spectrum. A belief for many that things are 100% right or 100% wrong means that tiny failures are viewed as complete failures. For many of us a 9/10 score on a test would be viewed as a success but some children will see not getting 10/10 as failure. As a teacher I see a positive result; a child who has good knowledge of the topic and the question that was incorrect directs me to a small learning gap to improve for next time. For a perfectionist they see failure and so what is the point of trying again as it will be the same result. As a teacher, too many children getting full marks shows me I haven't levelled the work correctly and I'm not pushing enough, it is an unsatisfactory outcome. For my perfectionist child full marks is the only satisfactory outcome.

So I have 2 choices;

1. I make the work easy enough to achieve full marks, encouraging the damaging belief that they can always achieve this in real life. It makes my life easier in the short term but without teaching the child resilience they will spend their adult life avoiding and giving up easily.

2. I challenge the belief system and teach the value of mistake making. Give children the understanding that mistakes are part of life and that knowing how to overcome them is a skill they need for the future. This is much harder for me as their teacher but gives them life skills for the future. The bonus extrinsic reward for my investment is a child far better equipped to sit those exams and better results.

> *"Being a perfectionist doesn't mean you get things right more often: it just means you're adversely affected by not getting things right."* Unknown

RILEY'S JOURNEY

Riley came to our school aged 9 despite us at the time having no primary provision because of his levels of aggression. He would bite, kick, hit, throw things and become very overwhelmed very quickly. He was from a deprived area but had a loving parent and settled home environment. He was wiry, scruffy looking but handsome with his beach blonde hair and bright blue eyes. He could switch from angel to demon in a heartbeat, he had to be first, he had to win and he had to be right. There was no negotiation and no wriggle room.

We could engage him in activities if he thought he would be successful, we could learn with him if it meant no writing and we could involve him with others if he was the best at the activity they were doing. There had been suspicions of ADHD with Riley when he came to us and the diagnosis was confirmed soon after he started. The medication that came with the diagnosis delayed his 0-100 speed enough for everyone to feel safer, Riley included. In my experience one of the hardest things for children with ADHD is that they often don't feel in control of themselves. The extra thinking time also gave us the opportunity to build a relationship and get to know him better. As we created safety we saw other behaviours but most importantly personality traits start to show themselves. The inflexibility of Riley's thinking, the lack of empathy and inability to see how his actions affect others. An ASD diagnosis was also added.

We had become better at identifying triggers and intervening to prevent dysregulation, we were even able to teach them to Riley. He still hated to lose but could now play with others without flying into a rage. He had lots of friends and had become a pleasant child to have in school. He still had his moments and could really hold a grudge, he didn't speak to me for 3 months because I stopped him going up a corridor and asked him to go a different way, but he had learned to understand himself and developed self control. Such was the progress made by Riley he was given the option to return to mainstream at the start of year 10. To which he replied in true Riley style 'What the f$#k would I want to do that for'!

Take that as a no thank you then!

We still had a huge barrier for his learning. He was exceptionally bright and it was easy to set him work he could get right. His English work was high quality but once it was done it was done, much to the English teachers exasperation and the difference between a potential A and a C. His artwork was degree level but if it wasn't exactly as he wanted it would be ripped up. The art teacher took to swiping work away from him just before he destroyed it and running away to hide it. The difference was that Riley could see the funny side of this now. He was recognising that it was a barrier for him and was letting us help. The thought of not getting 100% for exams was a painful one for him. Getting 98% in a test would mean focussing on the 2% and

> this made exams incredibly stressful. We had worked on stress management, we had built up his achievements and self belief and confidence but when you perceive anything less than 100% as failure, you enter an exam room knowing you will fail.
>
> It requires extreme courage to make yourself that vulnerable.

Riley didn't achieve the grades he was capable of, what could have been As were Cs but he had achieved more than enough to go to college. His final project in art had been a fascination with horror make up which had secured his A* and he went to college hoping for a career in special effects. He has continued to be successful and paid us many visits. He came a long way from the scruffy blond knee biter and is testament to the entire sequential approach but especially stage 5.

Changing a fixed mindset is as hard a task as I have ever experienced and it took years. We were lucky in a way to be able to start Riley's journey at 9 years old. Many children like him don't get the support until much later and we may not have had time to complete the process. Had the process started earlier he may never have needed our school. Had he wanted to, he would have completed his education in mainstream, he thrived in a mainstream college because he'd given the tools and the understanding of himself. We didn't do it **to** Riley, we didn't do it **for** him. We did it **with** him!

Chapter 13

BEHAVIOUR IS COMMUNICATION

I understand being proactive is expensive. There are those in education who question that behaviour really is communication, there are also those that acknowledge it but don't believe it can be understood successfully and those that say the children are too far gone for mainstream. The truth is that there will always be children who will need a specialist provision and what they have to offer but my experience is that a lot of the children I worked with shouldn't be there. Their behaviours were extreme and they weren't able to cope in mainstream now, because of failure and missed opportunities, but with the right interventions at the right time they would have succeeded.

Their behaviours hadn't been seen as communicating, nobody had looked at the underlying causes so children had been forced to find their own ways to cope. The ways they ask for support aren't always obvious and often they take up time but sometimes children have something really important to say but have a really strange way of saying it. Sometimes we have to decipher;

LEE'S TEST

Lee was socially awkward, stubborn as a mule and openly negative about school. He felt like nobody understood him and to a degree he was probably right.

Lee had had an unsettled week, it wasn't unlike him to be oppositional and withdrawn but more than usual. He had had an altercation with the Headteacher earlier in the day and was struggling to move past it. I met him in the corridor where one of the teaching assistants was struggling with him. I offered a change of face for Lee and tried to engage him in a conversation. It can be hit and miss but he liked superhero movies and a few days earlier we'd had a conversation about the Shazam film. On this occasion he was having none of it and was adamant I should send him home. When I said I didn't want to he said he'd get sent home. This was immediately strange to me because Lee wasn't adverse to absconding and if he really wanted to go he would have gone.

He had taken a screw about an inch long out of the wall and started to threaten to stab me with it. When I still wouldn't send him home he poked me with it. I still didn't believe he wanted to go so I called his bluff and I offered him the door. If he chose to go we would deal with that later but I wasn't going to send him. He continued poking me but without any force, Lee was capable of being quite violent but he wasn't being, it was like he was testing my response.

I asked him if he wanted to tell me something. The fact

> he didn't say no gave me my answer and I suggested going to my room. To my surprise he followed. We sat but he didn't speak. I let him sit quietly while I started to do some work on the computer but he started to mess with my phone, I shared an office with Debs and he started to mess with her stuff on her desk. I turned off my computer screen and looked at him "do you want to tell me something?" He said nothing but his eyes said something else. Debs, as she often did, read the room and made an excuse to leave.
>
> It is at this point he disclosed some significant safeguarding concerns!

It had all been a test to see if I was trustworthy enough to tell his secret to. He'd tested other people that day but they had focussed on the behaviour, for whatever reason my gut feeling was something significant behind it. Having prescriptive behaviour policies based on actions would have meant I had to challenge the threats, I would have had to demand or take the screw, I would have had to threaten consequences when he messed with equipment. There will be those reading who question my leniency, but if I'd reacted with challenge I would have escalated the situation and failed his test, he would have never made his disclosure.

The truth is that behaviour is a form of communication and we all speak it, sometimes we have to work a little harder to decipher it. It can be argued we have to stick to policies, it can be argued what message does it send to other children when they see Lee behave that way and nothing be done and it can be argued we don't have time for this kind of intervention, but that hour I invested in Lee that day means he talked to me, he trusts me and he's invested in me. I am part of the school that passed his test and now he is invested in the school. That hour that was out of class has meant so many more hours in class, a huge reduction in negative behaviour and so much more work produced.

Nobody can convince me that it is a wasted hour!

LET THEM FLY

All too often we support children by insulating them and doing things for them. We put off seeking funding for real support because they might be ok, we don't want a label or we know that without failing first we can't get a diagnosis or funding to support. If we do get a diagnosis, the high level of support is needed for the entirety of their school life, having it there often means avoiding stressful experiences. We often do this with the best intentions but doing for them, means not preparing them for the future or giving them the resilience to succeed when the support inevitably is removed.

Wouldn't it be better to give the support early and then withdraw it. As I write this and look back at my role I realise that the more successful I was the less I was needed. Children who I would spend hours and hours with at the beginning, would integrate, become part of the school family and I would no longer be needed. I'd be going to them rather than the other way round.

LISTENING TO ETHAN

The term one of a kind gets used too much but Ethan truly was. I've never met anyone like him before and I'm not sure I ever will again. I'm sure I will one day see him on TV. Confidence, showmanship and wickedly funny, but it wasn't always like that. At the beginning it was incredibly tough.

Never having felt safe in school, never having belonged and never feeling understood. School was a tough place for Ethan. Littered with misunderstanding and failure it filled him with anxiety and frustration. He would often get things wrong in and out of class but not understand why he had upset people. He hated anyone thinking bad of him but regularly added to this with failed explanations. I would often spend time unpicking and explaining situations. It was time consuming, deeply frustrating and at times felt pointless. However they never were, not only because it showed Ethan I was there for him, willing to listen and had his back but also because it gave me the clues I could cascade to staff to help them understand and adapt their practice to meet his needs.

My breakthrough with Ethan came when I bumped into him by chance, very distressed having been sent out of PE. My conversation with him went a little like this;

Me "Ethan you seem very upset about something can I help?"

Ethan "Everybody hates me"

Me "I'm sure that's not the case, tell me what happened?"

Ethan "I didn't get it"

Me "what didn't you get"

Ethan "I didn't get it and he sent me out"

Me "What didn't you get?"

Ethan "I didn't get it and when I said I didn't get it he said I was being silly"

Me "What were you being asked to do?"

Ethan "when I said I wasn't being silly and that I didn't get it he sent me out for answering back"

Me "Ethan can you stay here whilst I go and find out, I'm sure it's a misunderstanding"

I knew that if I pursued this in this way I would be going round in circles. When I spoke to the PE teacher he was teaching Badminton serving. The method of teaching for this was to practice serving at a target on the other side of the net rather than an opponent. Very common and taught this way in schools up and down the country. When Ethan had said he didn't understand, the teacher had repeated the instruction, then felt Ethan was trying to avoid and eventually felt he was disruptive enough to send out.

Ethan's eventual explanation connected the dots. Badminton was a game for two people who hit the shuttle back and forth. What is the point of hitting it over the net if there is nobody on the other side to hit it back. 'I don't get it' had nothing to do with what he was being asked but everything to do with why he was being asked to do it. Ethan had to know why he was being asked to do something and how it benefited him to learn it.

Knowing the importance of this to Ethan meant that I knew how to approach my conversations with him meaning less time going round in circles but most importantly I could share this information with staff to aid their own explanations of tasks. Hours spent with Ethan became minutes at a time, 5 times a day became 5 times a week, became 5 times a month. The intense support initially given to Ethan wasn't needed because we had understanding and empathy to support him better. We had a sequence of support to work through and he thrived. Staff knew how to work with him and it improved his academic performance. His confidence increased and the child who had had no confidence was rapping on corridors at break time, wowing other kids with magic tricks and having staff in stitches. He was far from perfect but a completely different child.

It took us until year 11 to get Ethan's ASD diagnosis. If we had waited for the diagnosis before supporting him he would never have completed school. He didn't need one to one support, to be insulated from situations and things done for him. He needed things explaining differently. A reasonable adjustment that could have been done early in his school life preventing all the negativity from ever happening.

Chapter 14

CONCLUSION

Lots has been said about gaps in learning and catching children up. I believe if we focus on academic catching up we risk causing ourselves a lot more problems than we solve. I believe a focus on well being with triage and a sequential approach will enable children to catch up naturally. A lot of negativity has been addressed towards 'recovery curriculums' and 'soft starts'. The idea is that children will want to return to normal and the focus will be on learning. Some educators are concerned that changing our systems to focus on well being will convince the children they are traumatised.

The truth is that it isn't about changing the school curriculum. It is about changing the culture and ethos. All children won't need something different, but many will. Whether we pick up where we left off or turn school into a large nurture room doesn't matter. Doing the same for everyone without finding out what they need is at best poor practice, at worst failing in our duty of care. I've tried to provide a scaffold to meet that need.

There will be a huge gap between our children's experiences, their desire to return and their readiness to learn. A belief shared by many in education is that there must be a sustained period focused on repairing the loss of safety, trust and belonging for children before we return the focus to academic standardisation. I would echo this because if we don't get the children back on an even playing field, we won't have equal learning potential and we risk creating more challenging behaviour and more masking of feelings than ever before.

I have advocated this sequential approach for vulnerable children for many years but I believe it can benefit everyone, I believe there is a place for it in mainstream and I believe that now we need it more than ever.

I've given lot's of reasons why I believe in the sequential approach and examples of how it worked with many children. Intense support to secure stages 1-3 if they were needed, then gradually take it away when they are more independent and have their own strategies. Stage 4 gradual support and group work. Stage 5 drip fed over time.

The work at the beginning saves work down the line, it's not about extra resources it is about more efficient use of the ones we already have. We could deal with the outcomes and fire-fight over and over, or we could invest in putting out and stopping it starting in the first place. I accept that it hasn't been tried in mainstream schools and would take a huge commitment. Things wouldn't change overnight and it isn't the silver bullet we so often look for, but I genuinely believe there are educators out there looking for another way and I believe that this could be it. Schools like Carr Manor are achieving miracles but it's been a long committed journey to get there.

Our success was always time dependent. Many children weren't as lucky as Riley was. They don't complete the journey and achieve close to their potential. So much time is needed to repair damage from where school went wrong that we don't reach stage 5. Astonishing work is being done up and down the country by alternative provisions in breaking down the causes of behaviour, understanding it and preventing it. It's true that these settings are the ultimate firefighters when they need to be, but this is a small part of the job they do. Fire prevention is where their real talents lie.

However so much time is lost trying to undo. Undo the feelings of worthlessness, undo the avoidance strategies and getting them to take off the masks. Often it's so late the building blocks for that child are so unsteady we have to knock it all down and start from scratch. Having to start the whole sequence again at age 12 when adolescence is kicking in and the world is upside down. Undoing those years of failure and changing belief systems needs time we don't have. We can get them as far as we can. I've given examples of many success stories but I'd be lying if I said they were all like that. Sometimes it's too late to turn it around and we just have to do the best we can.

The thing is though, if we could start the process before the failure. what an impact it could have. Children who don't have fear and don't wear masks. The majority of my career was spent trying to undo what has already been done because that is how education works, but if only we could acknowledge the work we would save ourselves down the line by intervening earlier. This book provides a scaffold and a model but the sooner we start the less undoing we have to do.

We have all of the blocks, let's build them!

ACKNOWLEDGEMENTS

With special thanks to those who helped along the way:

Dee, Michael and Mum for the help and advice on the book every step of the way.

Mike and Kerry, for taking a chance on someone as messy and disorganised as me to be a school leader and being two of the best mentors I could have ever hoped for.

Of course Eve for always supporting me, especially writing a book in what has not been the most conducive of times or environment.

Finally to Eliza Fricker for the illustrations used throughout.

ABOUT THE AUTHOR

Graham Chatterley is a former SEMH school leader who recently started his own training company. Having experienced a huge range of behaviour as both a Primary and Secondary teacher, Graham then settled in EBD in 2007, watching it go on to become an excellent SEMH provision.

Graham has led training for thousands of Educators in Warrington and the North West. Being part of leading and training the regional outreach team gave the opportunity to support mainstream schools with their most challenging pupils, many of whom were at risk of exclusion. This gave great insight into how successful practice in a specialist setting could be transferred to a large mainstream and this is advocated for in all of his training.

Graham favours ethos and culture over quick fix behaviour strategies and believes the adults play a pivotal role in the behaviour of the students. Teaching behaviour to children often means going against natural instincts and impulses we have as adults. By increasing understanding and empathy through training teachers about how the child's experiences have impacted their feelings and how that is what has driven the behaviours, it will hopefully change how those behaviours are perceived. Not only does this benefit the child in every way, especially learning, but it helps staff wellbeing.

Graham is the Director of Changing Perceptions Limited, where the training and support to schools is designed to do just that.

Printed in Poland
by Amazon Fulfillment
Poland Sp. z o.o., Wrocław